Introduction - The Agile Leader: Mastering the Art of Modern Management

Strategic leadership and management are pivotal elements that drive the success and direction of any organization. This book aims to dissect these complex concepts, providing readers with a thorough understanding that is both nuanced and applicable in real-world scenarios.

Strategic leadership transcends the traditional boundaries of leadership, embodying not just the capacity to direct but also the vision to inspire and the foresight to plan for the future. At its core, strategic leadership involves the formulation and implementation of major objectives and initiatives, taken on behalf of an organization's stakeholders, through the utilization of resources and the coordination of the organizational environment.

Strategic leaders are defined by their ability to foresee, envision, maintain flexibility, think strategically, and work with others to initiate changes that will create a viable future for the organization. They are not confined to top management but are present at various levels within the organization, each contributing to the strategic dialogue with their unique perspective.

Leadership can be classified along several dimensions—such as styles (autocratic, democratic, laissez-faire), processes (decision-making, communication, problem-solving), and personality traits (extroversion, agreeableness, openness). Each dimension adds a layer of complexity to the leadership role, affecting how leaders interact with their followers and how they are perceived within the organization.

Understanding leadership as a process highlights the dynamic and interactive nature of leadership. This perspective emphasizes that leadership is not a static position of authority but a continuous interaction between leaders and followers, shaped by the context in which it occurs, including the organizational culture, team dynamics, and external environment.

The concepts of power and influence are integral to understanding strategic leadership. Power is the capacity to effect or have influence over others' behaviors, perspectives, and actions, whereas influence is the exercise of that power to achieve desired outcomes.

The distinction between strategic and operational leadership is crucial. Strategic leadership focuses on long-term objectives and the broader organizational vision, while operational leadership deals with the day-to-day management and implementation of the organization's strategy. Both are essential for the organization's success, requiring a balance between visionary thinking and practical execution.

The alignment of individual and organizational goals is fundamental to strategic leadership. By establishing common goals, leaders can unify their teams, foster a sense of purpose, and encourage collaboration towards achieving shared objectives.

The relationship between leaders and followers is central to the leadership process. Effective leaders recognize the importance of this dynamic, striving to understand and meet the needs of their followers while guiding them towards the organization's goals.

Leadership involves not only the direct management of individuals but also the leadership of groups and the entire organization. Essential leadership skills include communication, decision-making, emotional intelligence, and the ability to motivate and inspire others.

Henry Mintzberg's framework of 10 managerial roles provides a comprehensive look at the different roles leaders and managers play within an organization. These roles are categorized into three groups: interpersonal (figurehead, leader, liaison), informational (monitor, disseminator, spokesperson), and decisional (entrepreneur, disturbance handler, resource allocator, negotiator). Each role highlights a specific aspect of the managerial function, from providing information and support to making key decisions and managing resources effectively.

In any organization, the relationships between leaders, followers, and the broader organizational context are complex. Effective leadership hinges not just on the capabilities of the leader but also on understanding and navigating these relationships. This section explores the dynamics of these relationships, focusing on demand, needs, contribution, and focus, to provide a nuanced understanding of how effective leadership can foster a collaborative and productive organizational culture.

The demands and needs within an organizational setting are diverse and often vary significantly between different groups and individuals. Leaders must be adept at identifying and understanding these varied needs to effectively guide their followers and meet organizational objectives.

- **Demands:** These are the explicit and implicit expectations placed upon individuals and groups within the organization. For leaders, demands can range from achieving specific performance targets to maintaining high levels of employee engagement. For followers, demands might include clarity in role expectations, support for personal development, and a need for recognition.

- **Needs:** While demands are often externally articulated, needs tend to be more intrinsic and can include psychological (e.g., the need for autonomy, competence, relatedness), physical, and emotional aspects. Understanding these needs is crucial for leaders to motivate their teams and create an environment where individuals can thrive.

Contribution refers to the input or effort that individuals and groups bring to the organizational context. Effective leadership recognizes and values the diverse contributions of all members, understanding that each individual's work and ideas are vital to the collective success of the organization.

- **Valuing Contributions:** Leaders who acknowledge and appreciate the contributions of their team members not only boost morale but also encourage a culture of innovation and shared responsibility. This approach fosters a sense of ownership among team members, leading to increased motivation and commitment to organizational goals.

- **Encouraging Participation:** Creating channels for open communication and feedback encourages team members to contribute their ideas and perspectives. Leaders play a crucial role in facilitating these discussions and ensuring that all voices are heard and considered.

The focus of an organization refers to its priorities and objectives. Strategic leadership involves aligning the organization's focus with its strategic goals, ensuring that all efforts are directed towards achieving these outcomes.

- **Aligning with Strategic Goals:** Effective leaders ensure that the organization's focus remains aligned with its strategic goals, even as external and internal environments change. This requires continuous assessment and adjustment of strategies and objectives.

- **Fostering a Shared Vision:** A key aspect of leadership is the ability to communicate a clear and compelling vision for the future. By fostering a shared vision, leaders can unite team members around common objectives, enhancing collaboration and driving the organization forward.

The dynamics of relationships within an organization play a crucial role in shaping its culture. Leaders who effectively manage these dynamics can foster a culture that is both collaborative and productive.

- **Building Trust and Respect:** Trust and respect are foundational to any effective relationship. Leaders can build trust by being transparent, consistent, and fair in their interactions with team members. Respect is cultivated by valuing each individual's contributions and by fostering an inclusive environment where diversity is celebrated.
- **Encouraging Innovation and Adaptability:** A culture that values innovation and adaptability is better positioned to respond to changes in the external environment. Leaders can encourage this by creating a safe space for experimentation, where failure is seen as an opportunity for learning and growth.
- **Promoting Engagement and Commitment:** Engaged and committed team members are more likely to go above and beyond in their roles. Leaders can promote engagement by connecting the work of individuals and teams to the larger organizational goals, making each person feel valued and part of something bigger.

The next section delves into the rich tapestry of leadership and management theories and styles that have shaped our understanding of organizational leadership over the years. Each theory and style presents a different perspective on how leaders can effectively guide their organizations, adapt to change, and influence their teams. By exploring these varied approaches, we gain insights into the multifaceted nature of leadership and the diverse strategies leaders can employ to achieve organizational success.

Transactional Leadership (Bennis and Bass)

Transactional leadership, as described by Warren Bennis and Bernard Bass, focuses on the exchanges that occur between leaders and followers. This approach is predicated on the notion that followers are motivated through rewards and punishments based on their performance. Transactional leaders are primarily concerned with maintaining normal flows of operations and are effective in stable environments where tasks are clear and structured.

- **Key Features:** Clear structure, reward and punishment based, focus on efficiency.
- **Applications:** Best applied in environments where tasks are routine and goals are clearly defined.

Transformational Leadership (Bass & Riggio)

Transformational leadership goes beyond managing day-to-day operations and aims to inspire and motivate followers to achieve extraordinary outcomes by transcending their own self-interest for the good of the organization. Bass & Riggio's model emphasizes the four I's: Idealized Influence, Inspirational Motivation, Intellectual Stimulation, and Individualized Consideration.

- **Key Features:** Inspiring vision, personal development, intellectual stimulation, considerate of individual needs.
- **Applications:** Effective in dynamic environments that require change and innovation.

Values-Driven Leadership (Gentile)

Mary Gentile's Values-Driven Leadership focuses on aligning organizational goals with personal and communal values. This approach emphasizes ethical behavior and decision-making, suggesting that leaders should guide their actions and strategies based on a core set of values.

- **Key Features:** Ethical decision-making, alignment of personal and organizational values, integrity.
- **Applications:** Particularly relevant in today's corporate world, where ethical considerations are increasingly at the forefront of business decisions.

Situational Leadership (Hersey & Blanchard)

The Situational Leadership model proposed by Paul Hersey and Ken Blanchard argues that there is no single "best" style of leadership. Instead, effective leadership is contingent upon the situation at hand. Leaders must adapt their style to the maturity level of the individuals or group they are leading, ranging from directive (high task, low relationship) to coaching, supporting, and finally, delegating as followers become more competent and committed.

- **Key Features:** Adaptability, assessment of follower's maturity, flexibility in leadership style.
- **Applications:** Useful in varied organizational settings, especially when dealing with teams of differing levels of maturity and competence.

Contingency Theory (Fiedler)

Fiedler's Contingency Theory posits that there is no one best way to lead. Instead, the effectiveness of a leadership style is contingent upon the context and the specific situation. The theory suggests that the leader's effectiveness depends on how well the leader's style matches the context.

- **Key Features:** Context-dependent leadership, leader's situational control.
- **Applications:** Encourages leaders to assess their style and adapt to the situational demands.

Additional Theories and Styles

- **Path-Goal Theory (House):** Emphasizes how leaders can motivate followers by clarifying the path to goals and removing obstacles to performance.
- **Ethical Leadership (Mendonca & Kanungo):** Focuses on leadership that is guided by respect for ethical beliefs and values, and for the dignity and rights of others.
- **Entrepreneurial Leadership (Roebuck):** Highlights the importance of innovation, risk-taking, and the ability to drive change for business growth.
- **Authentic Leadership (Goffee & Jones):** Advocates for leadership that is genuine and transparent, encouraging leaders to be themselves with skill.
- **Distributed Leadership (Gronn):** Proposes the spread of leadership roles within an organization, emphasizing teamwork and collaborative decision-making.

Leadership effectiveness is significantly influenced by the leader's ability to adapt their style to the specific needs of their organization and team members. This adaptability is crucial across different stages of organizational life cycles—start-up, growth, maturity, and decline—as well as in response to specific risks and challenges. This section explores how leaders can flexibly adjust their leadership approach to navigate these varying circumstances successfully.

Organizational Life Cycles

- **Start-up Phase:** In the early stages of an organization, a more directive and hands-on leadership style might be necessary to establish structure and direction. Leaders often need to be visionaries, setting a clear path forward while being deeply involved in operations. The focus is on innovation, rapid decision-making, and resilience to overcome the initial challenges of establishing the organization.

- **Growth Phase:** As the organization enters a growth phase, leaders may shift towards a more participative leadership style. This period is characterized by expanding operations, which requires leaders to delegate responsibilities, empower team members, and encourage collaboration. Leadership during this phase focuses on sustaining momentum, managing resources effectively, and fostering a culture that supports expansion.

- **Maturity Phase:** In the maturity stage, the organization requires a balance between maintaining established processes and seeking new opportunities for innovation. Leaders might adopt a transformational or situational leadership style to motivate and inspire employees, driving engagement and innovation within a stable environment. The emphasis is on optimizing operations and exploring strategic opportunities for growth or diversification.

- **Decline Phase:** Facing a decline requires leaders to be highly adaptive and possibly revert to more directive styles if radical change is needed. This might involve making tough decisions, such as restructuring or exploring new markets. Leadership in this phase is about crisis management, turnaround strategies, and revitalizing the organization to return to a growth path.

Leadership adaptability extends beyond the organizational life cycle to include responding to specific risks and challenges such as financial difficulties, health and safety issues, or significant changes in market conditions.

- **Health and Safety Risks:** In situations involving health and safety risks, leaders may need to adopt a more authoritarian style to ensure compliance with safety protocols and quick responses to emergencies. Clear communication and decisive action are crucial.
- **Financial Challenges:** Financial difficulties require leaders to be more analytical and pragmatic, focusing on cost control, efficiency, and identifying areas for financial improvement. This might involve a shift towards a more transformational leadership style to inspire and motivate the team through challenging times.
- **Market Changes:** Rapid or significant changes in the market demand leaders to be highly adaptable, embracing change and innovation. This could mean adopting a more entrepreneurial leadership style, encouraging creativity, and being open to experimenting with new strategies.

The concept of situational leadership, which emphasizes adjusting leadership style based on the maturity and competence of team members, is particularly relevant when adapting to different situations. Leaders need to assess the readiness of their team to take on responsibilities, providing more guidance and support to those who are less experienced and granting more autonomy to those who are more capable.

- **Assessing Team Maturity:** Understanding the development stage of individual team members and the team as a whole is critical. Leaders can then tailor their approach, from more directive methods with less experienced teams to more delegative styles as teams gain competence and confidence.
- **Flexibility in Leadership Approach:** The key to successful situational leadership is flexibility. Leaders must be willing to adjust their approach as the situation evolves, continually assessing the team's needs and the external environment to determine the most effective leadership style.

The ability of an organization to achieve its goals and improve performance significantly depends on the effectiveness of its leadership and management. This chapter delves into practical strategies and essential skills that leaders and managers can utilize to enhance organizational performance. By focusing on creating a compelling vision, building cohesive teams, effective communication, and robust performance management, leaders can foster an environment conducive to continuous improvement and high engagement.

A compelling vision provides direction and inspires employees to strive towards a common goal. It is the foundation for all strategic planning and a critical element of successful leadership.

- **Articulating the Vision:** Leaders must clearly articulate a vision that is ambitious yet achievable. This vision should resonate with employees' values and aspirations, motivating them to work towards its realization.
- **Aligning Vision with Action:** Beyond articulating the vision, leaders need to align it with actionable strategies. This involves setting short-term goals that are steps towards the long-term vision, ensuring that every team member understands their role in achieving these objectives.

Cohesive teams and effective communication are pivotal for organizational success. Leaders play a crucial role in fostering teamwork and ensuring open and transparent communication.

- **Fostering Team Cohesion:** Building a team that works well together requires understanding the dynamics of team interactions, recognizing individual strengths, and creating opportunities for team members to collaborate and build trust.
- **Enhancing Communication:** Effective leaders ensure that communication channels are open and accessible. They practice active listening, encourage feedback, and are clear and consistent in their messaging. This openness fosters a culture of trust and mutual respect.

Effective performance management is essential for improving organizational performance. It involves setting clear expectations, monitoring progress, providing feedback, and addressing performance issues promptly.

- **Setting Clear Expectations:** Leaders and managers must clearly define roles, responsibilities, and performance expectations. This clarity helps employees understand what is expected of them and how their work contributes to the organization's goals.
- **Monitoring and Feedback:** Regular monitoring of performance and providing constructive feedback are vital for continuous improvement. This should be a two-way process, where employees feel valued and listened to, and their contributions are recognized.
- **Addressing Performance Issues:** When performance issues arise, they should be addressed promptly and constructively. Leaders should focus on identifying the root causes of underperformance and work with the employee to develop improvement plans.

Motivation is a critical driver of employee performance and organizational success. An engaging environment that fosters learning, development, and recognition can significantly enhance motivation.

- Understanding Motivational Drivers: Different individuals are motivated by different factors, including recognition, achievement, personal growth, and meaningful work. Leaders need to understand these drivers and tailor their motivational strategies accordingly.
- Fostering Learning and Development: Opportunities for professional development and career growth are significant motivators. Leaders should encourage continuous learning, provide training and development opportunities, and support career advancement.
- Recognition and Rewards: Recognizing and rewarding employees for their contributions reinforces positive behaviors and outcomes. This can be through formal recognition programs, performance-based bonuses, or simple acknowledgments in team meetings.

Purpose of this book

This book is carefully designed to guide readers through the intricate landscape of strategic leadership and management within organizations, aiming to enhance organizational performance through the application of relevant skills and the effective utilization of teams. As you embark on this educational journey, here are the comprehensive learning outcomes you can expect:

Gain a Deep Understanding of Strategic Leadership and Management in Organizations:

- Grasp the pivotal relationship between strategic leadership and management and their collective impact on organizational success.

- Evaluate and compare various leadership and management theories, understanding their origins, development, and application in different organizational contexts.

- Adapt leadership and management styles to suit varying situations, including different stages of organizational growth, diverse team dynamics, and changing market conditions.

Enhance Organizational Performance through Leadership and Management Skills:

- Identify and develop the essential skills required by strategic leaders and managers to drive organizational performance and achieve strategic objectives.

- Understand and apply key motivational theories to influence organizational performance positively, recognizing the psychological underpinnings of motivation and how they can be leveraged to enhance employee engagement and productivity.

- Implement effective performance management strategies, appreciating their contribution to organizational improvement and the critical role of feedback, goal setting, and performance appraisals.

Leverage Teams to Improve Organizational Performance:

- Analyze the characteristics of high-performing teams, including the factors that contribute to their success and the challenges they face.
- Evaluate the role of a team leader in creating, maintaining, and leading high-performing teams, focusing on communication, conflict resolution, and motivation.

- Assess the impact of high-performing teams on organizational performance, understanding how effective teamwork can drive innovation, efficiency, and competitive advantage.

- Navigate the complexities of managing and supporting remote and/or virtual teams, developing strategies to maintain productivity, collaboration, and team cohesion in a digital work environment.

- Explore frameworks supporting effective team management and teamwork within organizations, applying these models to foster a culture of collaboration, trust, and shared success.

By the end of this book, readers will be equipped with a nuanced understanding of strategic leadership and management principles and their practical application in real-world scenarios. The knowledge gained will enable you to effectively lead and manage teams, drive organizational performance, and respond adeptly to the challenges and opportunities of the contemporary business landscape. This book aims not only to educate but also to inspire action and transformation, preparing you to make a significant impact in your professional endeavors.

Understanding Strategic Leadership and Management in Organisations

Concepts of Leadership and Management

Leadership and management, while often used interchangeably, serve distinct functions within an organisation. The terms embody different philosophies, methods, and outcomes. This section delves into the intricacies of these concepts, particularly focusing on strategic leadership.

Leadership vs. Management: A Primer

Leadership is about influencing others to achieve a vision or set of goals. It revolves around inspiring, motivating, and leading teams towards achieving broader organisational objectives. Leaders often challenge the status quo and are seen as visionaries.

Management, on the other hand, is about dealing with complexity. It involves planning, organizing, directing, and controlling organisational operations to achieve specific outcomes. Managers ensure that the day-to-day operations of the business run smoothly.

Defining Strategic Leadership

Strategic Leadership refers to a leader's potential to influence others to voluntarily make decisions that enhance the prospects for the organisation's long-term success while maintaining its short-term financial stability. It's about providing vision, direction, and purpose.

Characteristics of Strategic Leaders

- **Visionary:** They can see the bigger picture and understand how various elements come together to affect the organisation.
- **Adaptable:** They adjust strategies based on environmental changes.
- **Risk-taking:** They're not afraid to make bold decisions, understanding the balance between risk and reward.
- **Decisive:** When faced with difficult decisions, they act with clarity and speed.

Role of Strategic Leaders

- **Setting Direction:** Articulating a compelling vision and mission for the organisation.
- **Alignment:** Ensuring that resources, processes, and systems align with the strategic objectives.
- **Building Commitment:** Cultivating a unified team that is dedicated to achieving the set objectives.

- **Creating a Learning Organisation:** Promoting a culture of continuous learning and adaptation.

Significance of Strategic Leadership

- Long-Term Focus: Strategic leaders emphasize sustainable growth rather than short-term gains. They prioritize long-term objectives over temporary achievements.
- Cultivating Innovation: By challenging traditional ways of doing things, strategic leaders encourage innovation, fostering environments where novel ideas are heard and tested.
- Handling Crisis: In moments of crisis, strategic leaders exhibit calmness, providing guidance and direction to navigate through challenges.

Understanding the nuances between leadership and management is crucial for the effective functioning of any organisation. Especially in the realm of strategy, leadership becomes a pivotal force driving an organisation towards a prosperous future. While managers ensure the path is free of operational hurdles, strategic leaders ensure that the path being taken is the right one.

Classification of Leadership

Leadership, being multidimensional, can be classified in various ways based on different parameters, such as the dimensions or frameworks within which leaders operate, the processes they use, or the inherent personality traits they exhibit. This section will delve into these classifications to offer a comprehensive understanding of the diverse leadership styles and typologies.

Dimensions of Leadership

- **Transactional Leadership**
    - Focuses on exchanges between leaders and followers. Leaders provide rewards or punishments based on performance.
    - Often works on established procedures and guidelines.

- **Transformational Leadership**
    - Emphasizes inspiring and motivating followers to exceed their own limits and achieve the vision of the organisation.
    - Encourages creativity, personal growth, and development.

- **Laissez-Faire Leadership (Free-Rein Leadership)**

- Leaders provide minimal guidance to followers, granting them significant autonomy in how they accomplish their tasks.
- Effective where team members are highly skilled and motivated.

Leadership Processes

Task-Oriented Leadership

- Centers on the job, and is driven by an end goal.
- Leaders define roles and tasks, and provide tools, resources, and oversight required for task completion.

Relationship-Oriented Leadership

- Focuses on supporting, motivating, and developing the individuals in an organisation.
- More concerned with team dynamics, collaboration, and the well-being of team members.

Servant Leadership

- Leaders prioritize the needs of their team members before their own. They aim to serve rather than direct.
- Fosters a culture of trust, collaboration, and ethics.

Personality-Driven Leadership

- **Charismatic Leadership**
  - Based on the charm and persuasiveness of the leader.
  - Such leaders inspire enthusiasm in their teams and are energetic in motivating employees to move forward.

- **Autocratic Leadership**
  - Leaders make decisions unilaterally. They expect subordinates to obey without input.
  - Suitable in situations where decision-making needs to be swift without group consultation.

- **Democratic or Participative Leadership**
  - Leaders involve team members in the decision-making process, fostering collaboration.
  - Decisions might take longer, but the process is more inclusive.

- **Situational Leadership**

- Leaders adjust their style depending on the readiness or maturity level of their followers.
- It's flexible and considers the needs of the team.

Leadership, as a subject, is vast and multi-faceted. The various classifications above offer a lens to understand different approaches to leadership. Depending on the context, the culture of the organisation, the nature of the task, the personalities involved, and more, effective leaders might employ one or a combination of these styles. Recognizing the appropriate leadership style to employ in various situations can be a key factor in organisational success.

Leadership as a Process

Leadership is not just a static trait or a set of characteristics that an individual possesses. Instead, it can be understood as a dynamic process involving various elements, such as the leader, the followers, and the contextual environment. Let's explore leadership in-depth, as a continual process of influence.

The Nature of the Leadership Process

- **Dynamic Interaction:** Leadership is a reciprocal relationship between those who lead and those who choose to follow. The interplay between the leader's vision and the followers' acknowledgment is continuous.

- **Influence:** At its core, leadership is about influencing the behavior of others to achieve a certain objective or vision. It's not about authority or power but the ability to motivate, inspire, and guide others.

Components of the Leadership Process

a. **Vision Creation**
   - Leaders establish a clear vision for the future. This requires foresight, creativity, and the ability to dream big.
   - Effective leaders articulate this vision in a way that is both compelling and inspiring.
b. **Building Trust and Credibility**
   - Leadership is deeply rooted in trust. Leaders must demonstrate reliability, integrity, and authenticity to gain the trust of their followers.
   - Through consistent actions and transparent communication, leaders build and maintain their credibility.
c. **Communication**
   - Effective leaders ensure open channels of communication. This involves not only conveying messages but also actively listening to feedback.
   - Leaders bridge any potential gaps between strategy formulation and its execution through clear communication.
d. **Empowering and Developing Others**

- Leaders foster an environment where team members feel valued and empowered to take action.
- They provide opportunities for followers to learn, grow, and develop, often serving as mentors or coaches.

e. **Decision-Making**
- Leaders are responsible for making both strategic and operational decisions. This involves analyzing information, considering alternatives, and choosing the best course of action.
- They often have to make decisions under uncertainty and pressure, demonstrating resilience and adaptability.

f. **Adaptation and Change Management**
- As environments evolve, effective leaders are agile and can navigate through changes.
- They help their teams understand, adapt to, and champion change, mitigating resistance and fostering a culture of continuous evolution.

Influence of Context

- **Organizational Culture:** The values, norms, and practices of an organization can shape or constrain leadership processes.

- **External Environment:** Factors such as market dynamics, technological advancements, and socio-cultural changes can impact leadership decisions and actions.

- **Team Dynamics:** The interactions, relationships, and behaviors within a team can influence leadership styles and strategies.

Leadership, when viewed as a process, underscores the importance of ongoing interactions, continuous learning, and adaptation. It's an evolving journey wherein leaders and followers collaboratively move towards achieving common goals. By understanding leadership as a process, organizations can foster a dynamic and flexible approach to leadership, promoting sustained success and growth.

Power and Influence in Leadership

Power and influence are pivotal concepts in leadership. While they may seem synonymous, they function differently. Power is the capacity to cause change, while influence is the application of this power to effectively change behavior, opinions, or decisions. Understanding these concepts is essential for effective leadership, as leaders often rely on both to guide their teams and organizations.

1. Types of Power

Power in leadership can be derived from various sources

a. Legitimate Power

- Derived from a person's position or role within an organization.
- For example, a CEO or a manager has power because of their formal position.

b. Coercive Power

- Based on fear or the ability to distribute punishment.
- For instance, a leader might threaten job security to get an employee to act.

c. Reward Power

- Comes from the ability to confer valued rewards or positive incentives.
- Examples include bonuses, promotions, or praise.

d. Expert Power

- Based on skills, knowledge, and expertise.
- An IT expert in a company, for instance, would have power in technological decision-making.

e. Referent Power

- Derived from personal traits, charisma, or relationships.
- A leader who is respected and admired may have strong referent power.

Influence Tactics

a. Rational Persuasion

- Using logical arguments or factual evidence to convince someone.

b. Inspirational Appeals

- Tapping into a person's values or aspirations to drive behavior.

c. Consultation

- Engaging others in the decision-making process to build agreement and commitment.

d. Collaboration

- Working together to achieve a shared goal, thus ensuring buy-in.

e. Personal Appeals

- Asking someone to do a favor out of friendship or loyalty.

f. Exchange

- Offering something in return for cooperation, like a reward or benefit.

g. Pressure

- Using demands, threats, or intimidation to gain compliance.

h. Legitimating Tactics

- Asserting one's authority or referring to company policies to justify a decision.

i. Coalition Tactics

- Gaining the support of other people or groups to persuade someone.

Effective Use of Power and Influence

While leaders have access to various sources of power, ethical use of this power is crucial. Over-reliance on coercive power, for instance, can create a toxic work environment. Instead, leaders should seek a balanced mix, favoring referent and expert power to create an environment of respect and trust.

Similarly, while influence tactics can guide behaviors, they should be used responsibly. Manipulative or deceitful tactics can erode trust and harm a leader's reputation.

Strategic and Operational Leadership

In organizational leadership, understanding the distinctions between strategic and operational aspects is pivotal. While both are critical for the successful execution of an organization's goals, they operate at different levels, focus on varied time horizons, and employ different skill sets.

Strategic Leadership

> **a. Definition:** Strategic leadership refers to a leader's ability to express a strategic vision for the organization and motivate and persuade others to align with that vision.

Key Aspects

- **Visionary:** Strategic leaders often focus on long-term goals, shaping the organization's direction and purpose.

- **Big Picture Orientation:** They see the broader organizational landscape, anticipate future trends, and determine how the organization can capitalize on them.

- **Decision-making:** Strategic decisions involve significant resources and are long-term in nature.

- **Risk-taking:** As they're forward-looking, strategic leaders often need to take calculated risks.

Examples
- Deciding to enter a new market
- Launching a new product line
- Adopting a new technology ahead of competitors

Operational Leadership

Definition: Operational leadership focuses on the short-term aspects of an organization, emphasizing the execution of strategies set by strategic leaders.

Key Aspects

- **Detail-oriented:** Operational leaders are concerned with the day-to-day tasks of the organization. They ensure that processes run efficiently and effectively.

- **Problem-solving:** They often tackle immediate challenges and troubleshoot issues as they arise.

- **Performance Management:** Monitoring key performance indicators (KPIs) and ensuring that teams meet their targets falls under operational leadership.

- **Resource Allocation:** Operational leaders ensure that the organization's resources - whether human, financial, or material - are effectively utilized.

Examples
- Streamlining a production process
- Managing staff schedules
- Addressing a sudden drop in product quality.

Interplay between Strategic and Operational Leadership

While distinct, strategic and operational leadership are deeply interwoven:

- **Alignment:** Operational leadership ensures that daily activities align with the strategic vision set by strategic leaders.

- **Feedback Loop:** Operational leaders provide insights from the ground level that can inform strategic decisions.

- **Execution:** A brilliant strategy is futile without excellent operational execution. Conversely, efficient operations are directionless without a clear strategy.

Strategic and operational leadership, though different in nature and focus, are both crucial to an organization's success. Effective organizations often have a balance of both, ensuring they are not only visionary but also excel in execution. Leaders, regardless of their primary role, benefit from understanding both dimensions, ensuring that strategy is well-executed and that operations align with long-term goals.

The Importance of Common Goals in Organizations

Common goals serve as a foundation for collaboration and coordinated effort within an organization. They guide decision-making, focus resources, and unify team members, providing clarity and direction. In the broader context of organizational success and cohesion, understanding the significance of common goals is paramount.

Alignment and Direction

- **Unified Vision:** Common goals ensure that all members of an organization, from top management to the frontline employees, are on the same page and moving in the same direction.
- **Resource Prioritization:** When objectives are clear, organizations can more effectively allocate resources, such as time, manpower, and finances, to activities that directly support these goals.

Motivation and Engagement

- **Collective Purpose:** Shared goals foster a sense of collective purpose, boosting team morale and motivation.
- **Achievement and Reward:** When everyone works towards the same objectives, the sense of achievement upon reaching those goals is shared, creating a positive feedback loop that further motivates team members.

Accountability and Measurement

- **Clear Expectations:** Common goals establish clear expectations, allowing team members to understand their roles and responsibilities.
- **Performance Metrics:** Shared objectives provide benchmarks for performance. Progress can be tracked, and any deviations can be corrected in real-time.

Enhancing Collaboration

- **Cross-functional Synergy:** When different departments or teams have overlapping goals, they are more likely to collaborate, leading to cross-functional innovations and efficiencies.
- **Reduced Conflicts:** Shared goals can prevent or reduce inter-departmental conflicts, as everyone understands how their roles fit into the bigger picture.

Strategic Focus

- **Driving Strategy:** Common goals stem from an organization's overarching strategy, ensuring that daily activities and decisions align with long-term aspirations.

- **Adaptability:** Shared objectives provide a framework that, while focused, can also be flexible. As external factors change, organizations can adapt their goals while maintaining alignment with their overall mission.

Stakeholder Trust and Loyalty

- **Transparency:** Clearly articulated common goals offer transparency to stakeholders, be it employees, investors, or customers.
- **Trust Building:** When stakeholders observe an organization consistently working towards and achieving its shared goals, trust is reinforced, leading to increased loyalty and commitment.

Common goals are more than just organizational targets; they represent the collective aspirations of an institution and its members. They form the glue that binds individuals into a cohesive, focused, and effective unit. As organizations evolve and face new challenges, the continuous reaffirmation and adaptation of these shared goals become essential in navigating the path to success.

Leaders, Followers, and Group Leadership: The Dynamics and Required Skills

Understanding the dynamic interplay between leaders, followers, and group leadership is fundamental to effective organizational management. Leadership is not a one-dimensional concept confined to those in command; it encompasses the collective energy of both the leader and those they lead. This interdependence necessitates certain skills for holistic leadership effectiveness.

Dynamics of Leaders and Followers

- **Mutual Influence:** While leaders guide and influence their followers, the feedback and actions of the followers also shape leadership strategies and decisions.
- **Role Flexibility:** Effective teams often have members who can alternate between leadership and followership roles depending on the situation, bringing forward the most competent individual for a specific task.
- **Trust and Respect:** The foundation of the leader-follower relationship is trust. Leaders earn respect by being consistent, fair, and competent, while followers gain trust by being reliable and committed.

Leadership of Groups

- **Diverse Skill Utilization:** Leading groups requires leveraging the diverse skills and expertise present within the group to achieve collective objectives.
- **Group Cohesion:** Leaders must foster a sense of unity and belonging among group members to ensure collaboration and reduce conflicts.
- **Facilitating Participation:** Effective group leadership encourages active participation from all members, ensuring diverse viewpoints are considered.
- **Conflict Resolution:** Differences in opinion are natural in groups. Leaders need to be adept at mediating disagreements and finding common ground.

Essential Leadership Skills

- **Emotional Intelligence (EI):** Leaders with high EI understand and manage their emotions while also empathizing with the emotions of others. This fosters better interpersonal relationships and decision-making.
- **Communication:** Effective communication is crucial for conveying vision, setting expectations, and providing feedback.
- **Adaptability:** In a rapidly changing environment, the ability to adapt and respond to new challenges is vital.

- **Decision-Making:** Leaders need to make timely and informed decisions, often under pressure, that align with the organization's goals.
- **Delegation:** Effective leaders recognize the strengths of their team members and delegate tasks accordingly, ensuring efficiency and fostering trust.
- **Motivation:** Inspiring and motivating team members, acknowledging their contributions, and providing a clear vision can drive higher levels of performance and commitment.
- **Problem-Solving:** Leaders often face unexpected challenges and need to be resourceful in identifying and implementing solutions.
- **Strategic Thinking:** Beyond day-to-day tasks, leaders need to consider the long-term implications of their decisions and actions.

The art of leadership extends beyond the individual at the helm. It encapsulates the intricate relationship between leaders and followers and the nuances of leading groups. By honing essential skills and fostering an environment of trust, respect, and collaboration, leaders can guide their teams to success and ensure the sustained growth of their organizations.

Mintzberg's 10 Managerial Role

Henry Mintzberg, a renowned academic and author on business and management, identified ten managerial roles in his book "The Nature of Managerial Work" in 1973. These roles define a manager's activities in an organizational context. Mintzberg classified these roles into three categories: interpersonal, informational, and decisional.

Interpersonal Roles
These roles relate to the manager's responsibility for managing people and maintaining interpersonal relationships.

a. **Figurehead:** As the symbolic head, a manager has social, ceremonial, and legal responsibilities. They represent their organization or department.
b. **Leader:** Responsible for the work and performance of subordinates, providing direction, motivation, and a climate of trust.
c. **Liaison:** Establishes networks outside the immediate team, connecting with peers and others within and outside the organization. This is essential for gathering information and resources.

Informational Roles
These roles pertain to collecting, receiving, and disseminating information.

- **Monitor:** Constantly seeks industry and market information, keeping an eye on organizational issues and external trends that might affect the team or business.

- **Disseminator:** Ensures that the information is communicated effectively within the organization. This involves transmitting facts, expectations, feedback, and other insights.

- **Spokesperson:** Represents the organization to outsiders, relaying the company's plans, policies, actions, and results, and also negotiating on behalf of the organization.

Decisional Roles
These roles relate to decision-making processes and strategies.

a. **Entrepreneur:** Seeks to improve the organization, facilitating innovation and encouraging change.
b. **Disturbance Handler:** Takes corrective action during disputes or crises, resolving conflicts between subordinates or between the department and other groups.
c. **Resource Allocator:** Decides where organizational resources are best applied. This includes the allocation of funding, assignment of staff, and other critical decisions.
d. **Negotiator:** Represents the organization or department during negotiations of issues affecting managerial responsibilities.

Mintzberg's classification offers a comprehensive understanding of the multifaceted roles that managers play in organizations. By recognizing and understanding these roles, managers can better navigate their responsibilities and enhance their effectiveness. They also provide a lens for aspiring managers to understand the diverse capabilities they need to develop for managerial success.

Relationship: Demand, Needs, Contribution, and Focus

The relationship between demand, needs, contribution, and focus forms the bedrock of many organizational, societal, and individual contexts. Each component influences and interacts with the others, creating a dynamic interplay that drives decision-making, strategy, and operations.

Demand

Definition: Demand refers to the desire for a particular product, service, or resource, often coupled with the ability and willingness to purchase or acquire it.

Interaction

When there's a recognized need, it often translates to demand in the marketplace.

Demand might require an organization or individual to focus on certain areas, leading to specific contributions to meet this demand.

Needs

Definition: Needs represent fundamental requirements or deficiencies that people or organizations seek to fulfill.

Interaction

- Recognizing a need can lead to the creation or enhancement of a demand in the market.
- Addressing specific needs requires a focus on targeted solutions, which in turn dictates the type of contribution required.

Contribution

Definition: Contribution refers to the act of providing something, whether it's a product, service, knowledge, or resources, to fulfill a specific demand or need.

Interaction

- Contributions aim to meet the demand and needs of a target audience.
- The value of the contribution often requires a clear focus to ensure it's relevant and effective.

Focus

Definition: Focus pertains to the concentration of effort or resources on a specific task, area, or goal.

Interaction

- A sharp focus can help identify latent needs or predict future demands.
- Based on the focus, entities can tailor their contribution to be more impactful and aligned with market dynamics.

The intricate relationship between demand, needs, contribution, and focus forms a cycle of recognition, fulfillment, provision, and prioritization. Understanding these components and their interrelations is crucial for businesses, policymakers, and individuals to make informed decisions and create value.

Leadership and Management Theories and Styles

Transactional Leadership (Bennis and Bass)

Transactional leadership, as conceptualized by leadership experts like Warren Bennis and Bernard Bass, is rooted in the notion of "transactions" or exchanges between the leader and their followers. In this leadership style, the leader provides rewards or punishments based on the performance of the followers.

Key Characteristics

- **Contingent Reward:** Leaders set clear criteria for rewards. If employees meet their objectives, they are rewarded; if they fail, they may not receive the reward or may face consequences.

- **Management by Exception:** Leaders only step in when things go wrong. They monitor followers' performance and intervene only if standards are not met.

- **Task-focused:** Emphasis is primarily on completing tasks and maintaining workflow.

- **Reactive:** Transactional leaders typically respond to issues as they arise, rather than proactively seeking to innovate or predict future challenges.

Strengths

Clarity and Structure: Provides clear expectations and a straightforward reward system, making it easier for followers to understand their roles and what is expected of them.

Efficiency: Effective in situations where tasks are routine, and procedures need to be followed consistently.

Short-term Objectives: Effective for achieving short-term tasks and goals quickly.

Limitations

Lacks Emotional Appeal: This approach doesn't necessarily motivate followers intrinsically or inspire them beyond basic rewards.

Limited Innovation: May not encourage creativity or going beyond the call of duty, as the focus is primarily on established routines and achieving set targets.

Dependency: Over-reliance on rewards and punishments can create a culture of dependency, where followers only perform tasks to receive rewards rather than seeing the larger organizational vision.

Context

Transactional leadership can be effective in environments where processes are set, and consistency is crucial, such as manufacturing. However, in dynamic environments requiring innovation and adaptability, transformational leadership—a style that inspires and motivates followers towards a larger vision or goal—may be more appropriate.

Transactional leadership, while valuable in certain contexts, is just one of many leadership styles. Its efficacy largely depends on organizational context, the nature of tasks, and the characteristics of the workforce. Recognizing when to apply this style versus others is crucial for effective leadership and management.

Situational Leadership (Hersey & Blanchard, 1969)

Developed by Paul Hersey and Ken Blanchard in 1969, Situational Leadership Theory asserts that effective leadership is task-relevant, and the most successful leaders are those who adapt their leadership style to the maturity (readiness) of the individual or group they're attempting to lead or influence.

Key Components

Leadership Styles

- **Telling/Directing (S1):** Leaders make decisions and communicate them to followers. It's a one-way communication channel. Suitable for followers at low readiness level.

- **Selling/Coaching (S2):** Leaders still make decisions, but there's two-way communication. The leader "sells" their idea by allowing followers to buy into the process. Suitable for a moderate readiness level.

- **Participating/Supporting (S3):** The leader works with the team and shares decision-making responsibilities. Suitable for a moderate to high readiness level.

- **Delegating (S4):** Leaders are still involved, but decision-making is handed over to followers. Suitable for followers at a high readiness level.

Follower Readiness/Development Level

- **R1 (Low):** Followers are unable and unwilling or insecure.

- **R2 (Low to Moderate):** Followers are unable but willing or confident.

- **R3 (Moderate to High):** Followers are able but unwilling or insecure.

- **R4 (High):** Followers are both able and willing or confident.

Strengths

- **Flexibility:** Encourages leaders to treat followers as individuals, recognizing that everyone has a different level of knowledge and experience.

- **Clarity:** Provides a clear framework that helps leaders identify the best leadership approach based on a follower's readiness level.

- **Developmental:** It can be used as a tool to help evolve the skills and abilities of the team over time.

Limitations

- **Over-Simplification:** While the model identifies four distinct leadership styles, leadership can be more nuanced and complex in real-world scenarios.

- **Reliance on Leader's Judgment:** The effectiveness of the model is highly dependent on the leader's ability to correctly diagnose the maturity or readiness level of their followers.

- **Ambiguity:** The readiness levels might not always be clear-cut, and individuals can display characteristics of multiple levels simultaneously.

Context

The Situational Leadership model can be applied in diverse organizational settings and is especially useful in environments with varying task complexities and team maturity levels. It has been popular in training and development programs to cultivate adaptive leadership skills.

Hersey and Blanchard's Situational Leadership theory offers a practical framework for leaders to adapt their style based on the readiness of their followers. Recognizing when to employ each style and accurately assessing the maturity of the team are critical for the model's successful application.

Contingency Theory (Fiedler, 1960)

Fred Fiedler's Contingency Theory, proposed in 1960, posits that there is no one best way to lead. Instead, leadership effectiveness is contingent upon the interplay of the leadership style and the situation or context. According to Fiedler, leaders have a fixed leadership style, which means they need to be placed in situations that match their style for optimal effectiveness.

Key Components

Leadership Style

Fiedler believed that leadership style is fixed and identified two primary styles using the Least Preferred Co-worker (LPC) scale:

- **Relationship-Oriented Leaders:** These leaders prioritize interpersonal relationships and work best in situations with intermediate favorability.
- **Task-Oriented Leaders:** These leaders are focused on tasks and are most effective in either highly favorable or highly unfavorable situations.

Situational Favorability

This considers the degree to which a leader can determine what their group does and can obtain their commitment to it. It's determined by:

- Leader-member relations (quality of relationship between leader and followers)
- Task structure (the clarity and structure of the task)
- Position power (the power of the leader's position through rewards, punishments, etc.)

Strengths

- **Practicality:** Provides organizations with a way to evaluate the match between a leader's style and a specific situation.
- **Comprehensive:** Accounts for both the leader's disposition and external factors in evaluating leadership effectiveness.
- **Predictive Power:** Offers insights into predicting which leaders will succeed in specific scenarios.

Limitations

Fixed Leadership Style: The assertion that leadership style is fixed and cannot be changed is debated among scholars and practitioners. Modern leadership training often focuses on developing a range of styles.

Complex Assessment: Implementing Fiedler's LPC to determine a leader's style can be subjective and complex.

Situational Parameters: The theory's emphasis on just three situational variables can be seen as restrictive, as real-world leadership scenarios can be influenced by a plethora of factors.

Context

Fiedler's Contingency Theory can be useful for organizations when placing leaders in specific roles or teams, ensuring a match between the leader's natural style and the situational demands. It provides a framework to evaluate the fit between the leader and the context.

The Contingency Theory by Fiedler emphasizes the importance of both the leader's style and the situation in determining leadership effectiveness. While certain components of the theory are debated, it has been foundational in leadership studies, highlighting the idea that the best leadership approach varies depending on circumstances.

Path-Goal Theory (House, 1971)

The Path-Goal Theory, proposed by Robert House in 1971, posits that a leader's primary role is to clarify and set clear paths to help followers achieve their goals and provide necessary support and rewards. The theory is grounded in the idea that effective leadership is dependent on the match between a leader's style and the needs of the subordinate in relation to the work environment.

Key Components

Leadership Styles

- **Directive Leadership:** The leader gives clear guidance and directions on tasks, clarifying what is expected.

- **Supportive Leadership**: The leader is friendly and approachable, promoting a pleasant work environment.

- **Participative Leadership:** The leader takes into account the suggestions and opinions of subordinates before making decisions.

- **Achievement-Oriented Leadership:** The leader sets challenging goals, expecting subordinates to perform at their highest level.

- **Follower Characteristics:** Factors like needs, preferences, skills, experience, and locus of control can influence how a subordinate might react to a leader's style.

- **Task Characteristics:** The nature of the task, be it structured or unstructured, routine or complex, can influence which leadership style is most effective.

Central Premise

The leader should adopt a style that complements or supplements what is missing in the work environment, enhancing the employee's motivation, and, by extension, their performance.

Strengths

Flexibility: Path-Goal Theory encourages leaders to adopt different styles depending on the situation, promoting adaptability.

Focus on Followers: Emphasizes the importance of understanding followers' needs and preferences, making it more employee-centered.

Comprehensiveness: Integrates motivation principles from Expectancy Theory, adding depth to understanding how leadership can influence motivation.

Limitations

Over-Simplification: While it identifies four leadership styles, real-world leadership can be more nuanced and complex.

Reactive Not Proactive: The theory tends to be more reactive, suggesting leaders adjust based on situations, rather than being proactive.

Ambiguity: The best choice of leadership style isn't always clear-cut, and multiple styles might overlap in certain situations.

Context

Path-Goal Theory is particularly beneficial in diverse organizational settings where leaders need to adapt based on varying subordinate needs and task requirements. It emphasizes the importance of enhancing employee motivation for better outcomes.

House's Path-Goal Theory provides a framework that leaders can use to adapt their style to meet the needs of their subordinates and the specific situation. By focusing on both leadership behaviors and the characteristics of followers and tasks, it offers a holistic approach to effective leadership.

Transformational Leadership (Bass & Riggio, 2006)

Transformational Leadership, as conceptualized by Bernard Bass and further refined with Ronald Riggio, emphasizes the leader's ability to inspire and motivate followers to achieve more than what is typically expected of them. These leaders bring about significant change in individuals and social systems, transforming followers' values, aspirations, and elevating their potentials.

Key Components

Idealized Influence (Charisma)

- Leaders serve as role models that followers seek to emulate.
- These leaders are admired, respected, and trusted.
- They demonstrate a commitment to ethics and integrity.

Inspirational Motivation

- Leaders inspire and motivate followers by providing a clear vision and a sense of purpose.
- They set high expectations and demonstrate a commitment to goals and the shared vision.

Intellectual Stimulation

- Leaders challenge assumptions, promote innovation, and encourage followers to think creatively and solve problems.
- They stimulate and encourage creativity in their followers.

Individualized Consideration

- Leaders offer support and encouragement to individual followers.
- They pay attention to the individual needs for achievement and growth by acting as a coach or mentor.

Distinguishing Features

- **Beyond Transactions:** Transformational leaders go beyond managing day-to-day operations and cultivate employee potentials.
- **Change Agents:** These leaders are dynamic, visionary, and capable of driving change.
- **Engagement:** They involve themselves fully with their followers, making the group's interests a top priority.

Strengths

- **Higher Productivity:** Research has shown that transformational leadership can lead to higher levels of satisfaction, performance, and commitment among followers.
- **Adaptability:** Effective in various organizational settings and across cultures.
- **Positive Work Environment:** Promotes an enthusiastic and passionate work environment.

Limitations

- **Over-reliance on Charisma:** Too much reliance on the leader's charisma might overshadow other critical leadership skills.
- **Potential for Abuse:** The strong influence over followers might lead to exploitation.
- **Not Always Effective:** In routine-driven and highly structured environments, transformational approaches may be less effective.

Context

In dynamic environments where change is a constant, or in settings where innovation is pivotal, transformational leadership can be exceptionally effective. They are also essential during organizational turnarounds or in startups where a new vision needs to be articulated and passionately pursued.

Transformational Leadership, as articulated by Bass and Riggio, emphasizes the profound and expansive impact leaders can have on their followers. By inspiring, stimulating, and considering each follower's individual needs, transformational leaders can foster enthusiastic, dedicated teams capable of achieving remarkable outcomes.

Values-Driven Leadership (Gentile, 2014)

Values-Driven Leadership, as articulated by Mary C. Gentile in her work "Giving Voice to Values," refers to leadership that is guided by a set of ethical values and principles. Rather than just recognizing the right values, this approach emphasizes acting on them, especially in the face of opposition or challenges. It's about "knowing the right thing to do and getting it done."

Key Components

Self-Knowledge and Reflection

- Leaders must be clear about their core values and principles.
- Regular reflection to ensure decisions align with these values.

Preparation

- Anticipating the challenges and objections one might face when acting on values.
- Planning in advance how to respond and navigate these challenges.

Voice

- Developing the capacity to speak up effectively and assertively, not aggressively.
- Articulating one's values clearly and persuasively.

Support and Collaboration

- Seeking and cultivating supporters who share similar values.
- Collaborating to amplify the strength of values-driven initiatives.

Distinguishing Features

- **Action-Oriented:** Beyond just recognizing or discussing values, it emphasizes acting on them.
- **Proactive Approach:** Anticipates challenges and prepares for them rather than merely reacting.
- **Empowerment:** Provides tools and methodologies to empower professionals to act on their values.

Strengths

- **Sustainability:** By aligning actions with values, organizations can achieve long-term sustainability and stakeholder trust.

- **Ethical Culture:** Promotes an organizational culture where ethics and integrity are at the forefront.
- **Reduced Scandals:** Minimizes risks of ethical breaches and associated scandals or penalties.

Limitations

- **Resistance:** Encountering resistance from stakeholders accustomed to traditional ways of doing business.
- **Short-term Sacrifices:** Sometimes, values-driven decisions might not align with short-term profitability.
- **Ambiguity:** Differing interpretations of values can sometimes lead to ambiguity or conflict.

Context

Values-Driven Leadership is pivotal in today's business environment where stakeholders, including consumers and employees, increasingly prioritize ethical behavior and corporate responsibility. It's especially relevant for businesses seeking to build trust, enhance their reputation, and engage with socially-conscious stakeholders.

As introduced by Mary C. Gentile, Values-Driven Leadership doesn't just pose the question, "What is the right thing to do?" but pushes further with "How can I get the right thing done?" It equips leaders with the tools and mindset to act on their values, shaping organizations that are not only profitable but also ethical and responsible.

Ethical Leadership (Mendonca & Kanungo, 2007)

Ethical leadership, as conceptualized by Manuel Mendonca and Rabindra N. Kanungo, revolves around leading by moral values and demonstrating ethical behavior in both personal actions and interpersonal relationships. It's about integrating personal and organizational values to guide decisions, actions, and the behavior of followers.

Key Components

Moral Person

- Leaders showcase their ethical values and principles through personal behavior and decision-making.
- They possess honesty, integrity, and trustworthiness.

Moral Manager

- Ethical leaders proactively shape the organization's ethical context.
- They use rewards and discipline to guide ethical behavior among followers.

Role Modeling

- Leading by example is a central tenet of ethical leadership.
- Followers often emulate leaders, so the leader's moral actions set the standard.

Ethical Decision Making

- Decisions are taken based on a clear set of ethical standards, even when it's challenging or comes at a cost.

Stakeholder Interests

- Balancing the interests of diverse stakeholders, ensuring fairness, and avoiding bias.

Distinguishing Features

- **Holistic Approach:** Ethical leadership doesn't just focus on end goals but also on the means employed to achieve them.
- **Inclusivity:** Prioritizes the welfare of all stakeholders, not just shareholders.
- **Transparency:** Openness in decision-making and a willingness to share rationale.

Strengths

- **Organizational Trust:** Builds a deep-seated trust within the organization, which can improve morale and loyalty.
- **Risk Mitigation:** Reduces the risk of ethical scandals or breaches that can tarnish an organization's reputation.
- **Stakeholder Engagement:** Engaging ethically can result in better relationships with customers, employees, and other stakeholders.

Limitations

- **Complex Decision-Making:** Ethical considerations can sometimes slow down decision-making processes.
- **Conflict with Profit Goals**: Ethical choices might sometimes conflict with short-term profitability objectives.
- **Subjectivity:** Ethical standards can be somewhat subjective and open to interpretation.

Context

Ethical leadership is crucial in organizations that operate in sectors where integrity and trust are paramount (e.g., healthcare, finance, education). It's also vital in today's age, given the increased scrutiny from the public and media regarding corporate actions and responsibility.

Ethical leadership, as described by Mendonca & Kanungo, is an essential paradigm in contemporary leadership theories. In an era marked by corporate scandals and a clamor for increased transparency, ethical leaders serve as beacons, guiding their organizations through complex moral terrains, ensuring both profitability and integrity. They inspire trust, foster collaboration, and ensure that the organization's journey is as commendable as its destination.

Entrepreneurial Leadership (Roebuck, 2014)

Entrepreneurial leadership is an emerging leadership philosophy that blends traditional leadership characteristics with those of entrepreneurship. Roebuck in 2014 presented this style as one that combines risk-taking and innovation of an entrepreneur with situational awareness and motivational tactics typically employed by seasoned leaders.

Key Components

Innovation

- Central to entrepreneurial leadership is the drive to develop new ideas and methods.
- Constant search for opportunities to improve and grow.

Risk-Taking

- Willingness to take calculated risks to achieve desired outcomes.
- Embracing uncertainty as a chance to innovate and learn.

Vision

- Ability to envision a direction for the organization or project and inspire others to follow.
- Crafting a compelling story about the future.

Adaptability

- Flexibility in changing course when required.
- Continuous learning mindset.

Empowerment

- Trusting and empowering team members to make decisions.
- Encouraging autonomy and ownership.

Distinguishing Features

- **Opportunity-Driven:** Actively seeking out new possibilities and venues for growth.
- **Resilience:** A strong capability to bounce back from setbacks and use them as learning opportunities.
- **Boundary-Crossing:** Unlike traditional leaders, entrepreneurial leaders often transcend established roles, industries, or markets.

Strengths

- **Proactive Change:** Embracing change as a constant, thus positioning the organization ahead of market shifts.
- **Culture Building:** Encourages a culture of innovation, ownership, and calculated risk-taking.
- **Growth Focus:** Has an inherent growth mindset which can propel the organization to higher levels of success.

Limitations

Potential Overextension: In the pursuit of multiple opportunities, there's a risk of overextension or loss of focus.

Tolerance for Failure: While failure is often seen as a learning opportunity, too many failures can be detrimental to morale and resources.

Balancing Risk and Reward: There's always a need to strike a balance between taking risks and ensuring stable operations.

Context

Entrepreneurial leadership is especially potent in startup environments and industries experiencing rapid change. This leadership style is also making its way into traditional businesses where leaders recognize the value of agility, innovation, and adaptability in the face of the evolving market landscape.

Roebuck's concept of entrepreneurial leadership encapsulates the dynamism required in today's fast-paced business environment. Leaders who can harness the proactive, innovative, and risk-embracing nature of an entrepreneur, while also guiding and motivating a team, are positioned to thrive in contemporary business ecosystems. This style of leadership can catalyze growth, foster innovation, and drive organizations toward a prosperous future.

Authentic Leadership (Goffee & Jones, 2011)

Authentic leadership is grounded in self-awareness and genuine behavior. Leaders are true to themselves and promote openness and transparency. Goffee & Jones, in their 2011 work, emphasized the importance of leaders being themselves, but more skillfully, suggesting that authenticity isn't about showing every aspect of oneself, but revealing and amplifying certain qualities.

Key Components

Self-Awareness

- Understanding one's strengths, weaknesses, motivations, and emotions.
- Reflecting and acting upon feedback.

Relational Transparency

- Open, honest, and straightforward interactions.
- Sharing one's thoughts and feelings while being receptive to others.

Balanced Processing

- Fairly considering all relevant data and feedback before making decisions.
- Avoiding bias in decision-making.

Internalized Moral Perspective

- Guided by strong internal moral compass and values.
- Acting consistently with one's beliefs and values.

Distinguishing Features

- Consistency: Authentic leaders remain true to their personality and character in various situations, resisting the urge to project a false image.
- Ethical Grounding: Morality and ethics play a vital role in decisions and actions.
- Connection: Fosters deep and genuine connections with followers by being vulnerable and open.

Strengths

- **Trust Building:** Authenticity breeds trust, as followers believe leaders will act in consistent, moral ways.

- **High Engagement:** Teams led by authentic leaders tend to have higher engagement levels and satisfaction.
- **Ethical Decision-Making:** Decisions are grounded in values and ethics, promoting a strong organizational moral compass.

Limitations

- **Misinterpretation:** Being oneself can sometimes be seen as a lack of adaptability or incompatibility in some organizational cultures.
- **Over-Transparency:** There's a risk of oversharing or being too open, which can blur professional boundaries.
- **Challenge in Execution:** Being authentic is easier said than done, especially under pressure or in challenging situations.

Context

Authentic leadership thrives in organizations that value transparency, ethical behavior, and genuine relationships. It's especially relevant in today's business world, where trust in leaders is paramount, and inauthentic behaviors can be easily spotted and criticized.

Goffee & Jones' emphasis on authentic leadership illuminates the importance of genuineness in leadership roles. Such leaders not only create an environment of trust and openness but also drive ethical actions and decisions. They remind us that, while skills can be learned, true leadership emanates from one's core values and character.

Distributed Leadership (Gronn, 2000)

Distributed leadership, as articulated by Gronn in 2000, posits that leadership is not the province of a single individual, but rather a shared process among members of a group or organization. It emphasizes the collaborative and emergent nature of leadership, wherein multiple members take on leadership tasks in an intertwined manner.

Key Components

Concertive Action

- Leadership as a collective activity where tasks and functions are shared across members.

Co-Performance

- Shared tasks, where two or more individuals collaborate directly on a specific leadership task.

Spontaneous Collaboration

- Unplanned, emergent leadership actions that arise in response to immediate needs.

Institutionalized Practices

- Established routines, procedures, and norms that distribute leadership roles and responsibilities.

Distinguishing Features

- **Fluid Roles:** In distributed leadership, roles are flexible. Today's follower could be tomorrow's leader based on the situation and the skills required.
- **Emergent Leadership:** Leadership emerges as a result of interaction rather than hierarchies.
- **Interdependence:** It stresses the interdependence of team members and values collective goals over individual accolades.

Strengths

Adaptability: Organizations can become more agile, responding quickly to changes or challenges.

Utilization of Skills: Skills and talents of a wider group are harnessed, not just those at the top.

Shared Responsibility: The burden of leadership doesn't fall on a single individual, leading to shared ownership of outcomes, both good and bad.

Limitations

- **Lack of Clarity:** In the absence of clear roles, there might be confusion or overlap in responsibilities.
- **Potential for Conflict:** Multiple leaders might have differing opinions, leading to potential conflicts.
- **Requires a Collaborative Culture:** For distributed leadership to work effectively, an organization needs a strong culture of collaboration and trust.

Context

Distributed leadership is particularly effective in environments that are dynamic and require a high degree of adaptability. It's also beneficial in settings where collaboration and team work are emphasized, such as education, agile tech teams, and project-based tasks.

Gronn's concept of distributed leadership challenges traditional hierarchical models by emphasizing that leadership is a group quality rather than an individual trait. It advocates for a more democratic and collaborative approach, where leadership responsibilities are spread across individuals, harnessing the collective strengths of the group. This approach recognizes that in the complexities of modern organizations, no single person holds all the answers or skills.

Managerial Grid (Blake and Mouton, c.1950s)

Developed by Robert Blake and Jane Mouton in the 1950s, the Managerial Grid Model (also known as Leadership Grid or Grid Theory) offers a framework for understanding different leadership styles based on two key dimensions: concern for production (task orientation) and concern for people (relationship orientation).

Key Dimensions

Concern for Production

This refers to how much a leader prioritizes achieving organizational tasks and results.

Concern for People

This signifies how much a leader values interpersonal relationships, the well-being of team members, and their needs.

Five Major Leadership Styles

- **Impoverished Leadership (1,1):**
  - Low concern for both production and people.
  - Leaders display minimal effort, leading to a lack of motivation and commitment among team members.

- **Country Club Leadership (1,9):**
  - High concern for people but low concern for production.
  - Leaders emphasize team well-being and interpersonal relationships over output, which can lead to a comfortable, friendly environment but possibly lacking in discipline and productivity.

- **Produce or Perish Leadership (9,1):**
  - High concern for production but low concern for people.
  - Often seen as autocratic, these leaders prioritize results above all else, which can lead to high productivity but also high turnover and dissatisfaction among employees.

- **Middle-of-the-Road Leadership (5,5):**
  - Balanced concern for both people and production.
  - These leaders try to compromise, aiming for adequate results and adequate employee satisfaction but might not excel in either.

- **Team Leadership (9,9):**
  - High concern for both production and people.
  - Leaders motivate employees to perform at their best while also fostering a collaborative, supportive environment. This style is often considered ideal as it aims for both high productivity and high satisfaction.

Strengths

- **Versatility:** The grid offers a clear visual representation of leadership styles, allowing leaders to reflect on their style and adapt as needed.

- **Comprehensive Framework:** It addresses both task and relationship orientations, encompassing a broad spectrum of leadership behaviors.

Limitations

- **Over-Simplification:** Real-world leadership can be more nuanced than the grid's binary dimensions suggest.

- **Static Representation:** Leadership styles may need to adapt based on specific situations, which the grid doesn't inherently account for.

Context

The Managerial Grid is especially valuable for leadership training and development. By identifying their position on the grid, leaders can gain insights into their strengths and areas for improvement. The ultimate goal for many is to move towards the Team Leadership style, balancing both task and people concerns effectively.

Blake and Mouton's Managerial Grid remains a seminal model in leadership studies, providing a straightforward way to conceptualize and discuss leadership behaviors. It serves as a reminder that effective leadership often requires a balance between achieving tasks and nurturing team relationships.

Leadership Continuum (Tannenbaum and Schmidt, 1958)

The Leadership Continuum model, proposed by Robert Tannenbaum and Warren H. Schmidt in 1958, presents a range of leadership behaviors along a continuum. This model outlines the relationship between the degree of freedom a manager chooses to give to a team and the level of authority they use. It was one of the earliest models to recognize that leadership behavior is not a fixed point, but can vary according to the situation and individuals involved.

Key Components

Tell (Autocratic Behavior)

- Leader makes the decision and announces it.
- This approach is directive and based on the leader's own judgment and expertise.

Sell

- Leader makes the decision but attempts to gain commitment from the team by "selling" the benefits of the decision.

Consult (Two Sub-Styles)

Leader presents the problem, gets suggestions, then makes a decision:

- The decision is still very much in the leader's hands, but input is sought.

Leader presents a tentative decision that is subject to change and invites questions:

- The leader has a decision in mind but seeks validation or potential modifications.

Join

- Leader defines the limits and then collaborates with the team to arrive at a joint decision.
- The final choice is made together with the team.

Delegate

- Leader allows the team to make decisions within prescribed limits.
- The leader provides the boundaries but then steps back, allowing the team to decide.

Factors Influencing Leadership Style

- **Leader's Confidence in the Team:** Trust in the team's abilities can influence how much decision-making freedom is granted.
- **Leader's Personal Inclination:** Some leaders are naturally more autocratic or democratic in their approach.
- **Nature of the Task:** Routine tasks might not require as much team input as complex, novel tasks.
- **Organizational Culture:** A company that values innovation and creativity might lean towards more democratic leadership styles.
- **Team's Expectations:** If a team is used to autonomy, suddenly imposing a highly directive style might be counterproductive.
- **Urgency of the Situation:** In crisis situations, there might not be time for extensive consultation.

Strengths

- **Flexibility:** The model acknowledges that different situations and teams might require different leadership styles.
- **Broad Range:** It captures a wide spectrum of leadership behaviors, from autocratic to fully democratic.

Limitations

- **Lack of Specific Guidance:** While the model provides a spectrum, it doesn't offer specific advice on when to adopt each style.
- **Over-Simplification:** Real-world leadership situations can be more nuanced than the continuum suggests.

Context

The Leadership Continuum is particularly valuable in leadership development and training. By understanding the continuum, leaders can consciously adapt their style based on the situation and the people involved, leading to more effective management outcomes.

Tannenbaum and Schmidt's Leadership Continuum offers a dynamic view of leadership styles. It underscores the importance of situational adaptability in leadership and emphasizes that effective leadership is not about sticking to one style but about fluidly moving along the continuum as circumstances dictate.

Leadership Qualities (Bennis, 1989)

Warren Bennis, a recognized leadership scholar, has studied leadership extensively and has identified several key qualities that effective leaders possess. In his 1989 book "On Becoming a Leader," Bennis outlined essential qualities and differences between leaders and managers. Here's a comprehensive overview of the qualities Bennis attributed to effective leadership:

Vision and Purpose

- **Description:** Leaders have a clear understanding of what they want to achieve in the long-term. They have a compelling vision that drives them forward and inspires others to follow.
- **Significance:** A clear vision provides direction, meaning, and purpose for the entire organization. It offers a roadmap for where the leader and the team are headed.

Self-Knowledge

- **Description:** Effective leaders have an acute awareness of their strengths, weaknesses, desires, and motives. They engage in regular self-reflection and introspection.
- **Significance**: Understanding oneself allows a leader to capitalize on strengths, work on weaknesses, and ensure that their actions align with their core values.

Constant Learning

- **Description:** Leaders are lifelong learners. They seek to learn from experiences, challenges, failures, and successes.
- **Significance:** Continuous learning enables leaders to adapt to changing environments, make informed decisions, and foster innovation.

Authenticity

- **Description:** Leaders are genuine and true to themselves. They don't pretend to be someone they're not.
- **Significance:** Authenticity builds trust, credibility, and rapport with followers. People are more inclined to follow leaders who are real and relatable.

Adaptability

- **Description:** Leaders can adjust to new conditions, challenges, and environments. They're resilient in the face of change.

- **Significance:** The business world and broader environment are always evolving. Leaders who can adapt are better poised to navigate uncertainties and lead their teams through change.

Foster Trust

- **Description:** Leaders create environments where honesty, integrity, and reliability are valued and practiced.
- **Significance:** Trust is the foundation of any relationship, including those in an organizational setting. When team members trust their leader, they're more motivated, committed, and productive.

Drive and Passion

- **Description:** Leaders have an intrinsic motivation that fuels their drive. They're passionate about what they do.
- **Significance:** Passionate leaders ignite enthusiasm in their teams, creating an environment where people are motivated to meet and exceed their goals.

Ability to Communicate

- **Description:** Leaders can articulate their vision, ideas, and values in ways that resonate with others.
- **Significance:** Effective communication ensures everyone is on the same page, reducing misunderstandings and enhancing teamwork.

Warren Bennis's insights into leadership qualities provide a holistic understanding of what it takes to be an effective leader. Rather than focusing solely on skills, Bennis emphasizes the importance of character, self-awareness, and personal growth in leadership. Aspiring leaders can use these qualities as a roadmap for personal and professional development.

Leadership Styles (Goleman, 1995)

In 1995, Daniel Goleman, a psychologist and science journalist, introduced six leadership styles in the Harvard Business Review. These styles were based on emotional intelligence and highlighted how leaders could harness their emotions to drive particular organizational outcomes. Each style has its unique characteristics, advantages, and potential drawbacks:

Coercive (or Directive) Leadership

- **Description:** This style is characterized by demands and compliance. The leader gives orders and expects them to be followed without question.
- **Best Used:** In crisis situations where immediate compliance is required.
- **Drawbacks:** Can stifle innovation and can demotivate employees if used excessively.

Authoritative (or Visionary) Leadership

- **Description:** Visionary leaders provide a clear direction by articulating a vision and guiding their team towards it. They give the "why" behind each task.
- **Best Used:** When a new direction or vision is required.
- **Drawbacks:** May not be effective if the leader is not seen as credible.

Affiliative Leadership

- **Description:** This style prioritizes people over tasks. Leaders using this style promote harmony, build emotional bonds, and make their teams feel valued.
- **Best Used:** To heal rifts in a team, motivate during stressful circumstances, or strengthen connections.
- **Drawbacks:** Can result in mediocre performance if the leader only gives positive feedback and avoids addressing poor performance.

Democratic Leadership

- **Description:** Democratic leaders prioritize participation and collaboration. They seek input and feedback from their team members before making decisions.
- **Best Used:** When the leader needs the team's buy-in or when gathering diverse perspectives.
- **Drawbacks:** Can be time-consuming and may not yield optimal results if the team lacks the necessary expertise.

Pacesetting Leadership

- **Description:** Pacesetters set high standards for themselves and expect the same from their team members. They push their team to achieve excellence.

- **Best Used:** With motivated and skilled teams who need little direction.

- **Drawbacks:** Can be overwhelming for team members, leading to burnout and reduced morale.

Coaching Leadership

- **Description:** Leaders using the coaching style focus on personal development. They guide team members, provide feedback, and help them improve and develop their skills.

- **Best Used:** When team members are looking to build long-term capabilities.

- **Drawbacks:** May not be effective if the team member is resistant to learning or if the leader lacks expertise.

Goleman's leadership styles underscore the idea that effective leadership is not about adopting a single style but rather about flexibly adapting one's style based on the situation, the needs of the organization, and the team's requirements. By understanding and mastering these styles, leaders can better navigate diverse challenges and drive their organizations towards success.

Adapting Leadership Styles to Different Situations

Lifecycle of an Organisation:

Different stages of an organisation's lifecycle demand distinct leadership styles and approaches. Each phase presents unique challenges and opportunities.

Start-Up

- **Characteristics:** Rapid change, high uncertainty, resource constraints, need for agility, and market positioning.

Effective Leadership Styles

- **Visionary Leadership:** A clear vision can motivate early employees and provide direction.
- **Entrepreneurial Leadership:** Innovative, risk-taking leadership can capture opportunities and navigate uncertainties typical of a start-up.
- **Coaching Leadership:** Helps onboard new employees, aligning them with the company's culture

Growth

- **Characteristics:** Expansion, hiring surges, scaling operations, increasing revenue, and market penetration.

Effective Leadership Styles

- **Pacesetting Leadership:** Drives teams to meet growth targets and high-performance standards.
- **Democratic Leadership:** Engages a growing employee base, ensuring everyone feels part of the company's evolution.
- **Affiliative Leadership:** Promotes harmony and builds emotional bonds amid the pressures of growth.

Maturity

- **Characteristics:** Stable revenue streams, established market presence, operational efficiency, and increased competition.

Effective Leadership Styles

- **Transactional Leadership:** Emphasizes processes, procedures, and efficiency.

- **Authoritative Leadership:** Provides clear direction in a crowded market, ensuring the organization remains focused.
- **Distributed Leadership:** Empowers various departments or teams to take charge of their domains, fostering a sense of ownership and specialization.

Decline

- **Characteristics:** Falling revenues, market share loss, cost-cutting, and potential restructuring.

Effective Leadership Styles

- **Directive (Coercive) Leadership:** Ensures quick decision-making in crisis scenarios, possibly averting further decline.
- **Transformational Leadership:** Re-energizes and renews the vision and direction of the company.
- **Situational Leadership:** Adapts to rapidly changing scenarios, making real-time decisions based on immediate challenges and opportunities.

The lifecycle stage of an organisation significantly influences the leadership style that will be most effective. Leaders who can discern their organisation's lifecycle stage and adapt their style accordingly are better positioned to guide their teams to success. They not only understand the internal dynamics of their organisation but also the external market forces, allowing them to pivot and adjust their strategies as needed.

Adapting Leadership Styles in Response to Specific Risks

Organizations inevitably encounter risks, and effective leadership requires adapting to these risks to navigate challenges successfully. The type of risk will often dictate the necessary leadership style.

Health and Safety Risks

- **Characteristics:** Concerns related to employee well-being, workplace hazards, and potential for injury or illness.

Effective Leadership Styles

- **Directive (Coercive) Leadership:** Immediate action and strict compliance are essential. Leaders set clear safety protocols and ensure they're followed.
- **Democratic Leadership:** Engages employees in discussions about safety protocols, seeking their input and feedback to ensure a comprehensive understanding and buy-in.
- **Servant Leadership:** Prioritizes the well-being of team members, ensuring they have the resources and knowledge to stay safe.

Financial Risks

- **Characteristics:** Potential for financial losses, market downturns, investment concerns, and budgetary constraints.

Effective Leadership Styles

- **Pragmatic Leadership:** Focuses on practical solutions and strategies to navigate financial challenges, making difficult decisions based on the best available data.
- **Transformational Leadership:** Inspires and motivates the team during financially challenging times, fostering a culture of innovation and adaptability.
- **Transactional Leadership:** Emphasizes accountability and oversight, ensuring that financial protocols and standards are adhered to.

Strategic Risks (e.g., market competition, disruptive technologies)

- **Characteristics:** Threats that can alter the landscape of the industry or the position of the company within that industry.

Effective Leadership Styles

- **Visionary Leadership:** Looks ahead to anticipate market shifts and sets a clear direction for the organization to navigate them.

- **Adaptive Leadership:** Promotes a culture of flexibility, encouraging the organization to evolve and adapt in the face of emerging challenges.

- **Entrepreneurial Leadership:** Encourages innovation and risk-taking to capitalize on new opportunities or to pivot in response to threats.

Reacting to specific risks requires leaders to be both vigilant and adaptable. They need to constantly assess their environment, internal and external, and shift their leadership approach as necessary. By matching the leadership style to the nature of the risk, leaders can guide their organizations to resilience and success even in the face of adversity.

Objectives and Strategy in Leadership

Objectives and strategy serve as the backbone of an organization's direction and vision. Leadership's primary responsibility is to define these objectives and design strategies to achieve them. Let's delve deeper into their interconnected roles.

Objectives in Leadership

- **Definition:** Objectives are specific, measurable goals that an organization intends to achieve within a set timeframe.

Role in Leadership

- **Direction Setting:** Objectives provide a clear direction, ensuring that every team member understands what the organization is aiming for.
- **Performance Measurement:** By setting objectives, leaders can measure progress and determine if the organization is on the right track.
- **Motivation:** Clear objectives provide team members with a sense of purpose and motivation, as they understand the contribution they are making.

Strategy in Leadership

- **Definition:** Strategy is the high-level plan devised to achieve organizational objectives, considering the resources available and external challenges.

Role in Leadership

- **Guiding the Path:** Strategy acts as the roadmap, guiding the organization on how to move from its current position to its desired future state.
- **Resource Allocation:** Strategy helps leaders determine where to allocate resources, including capital, human resources, and technology.
- **Risk Management:** Effective strategy considers potential risks and includes contingency plans to address them.

The Interplay Between Objectives and Strategy

- **Alignment:** For a strategy to be successful, it must be aligned with the organization's objectives. This ensures that all efforts are directed towards goal achievement.
- **Adaptability:** While objectives provide a stable target, strategies may need to adapt in response to internal and external changes. Leaders must be agile in re-evaluating and adjusting strategies while keeping the core objectives intact.

- **Feedback Loop:** The results achieved from implementing a strategy provide feedback on the relevancy and appropriateness of the objectives. Sometimes, achieving a strategy might lead to redefining objectives based on new insights and environmental changes.

Effective leadership recognizes the importance of clear objectives and well-thought-out strategies. While objectives set the destination, strategy plots the course. Leaders must continuously monitor and adjust both, ensuring that the organization remains aligned with its vision and mission. Through this dynamic interplay, organizations can navigate challenges, capitalize on opportunities, and achieve sustained success.

Responding to Customer Demands in Leadership

In today's customer-centric business environment, responding to customer demands is pivotal. Leadership plays a vital role in ensuring an organization remains adaptable, responsive, and in tune with its customers' needs and preferences. Let's explore how leadership can effectively address customer demands.

Recognizing the Importance of Customers

- **Centrality of Customers:** Effective leaders understand that customers are the lifeblood of any business. Without meeting their demands, businesses risk obsolescence.
- **Continuous Feedback:** Leaders prioritize systems that gather continuous feedback from customers, ensuring that they have a pulse on what customers desire and expect.

Cultivating a Customer-centric Culture

- **Emphasizing Empathy:** Leaders promote a culture where every team member is encouraged to understand and empathize with customer needs.
- **Rewarding Responsiveness:** Employees who go the extra mile to address customer demands are recognized and rewarded, reinforcing a customer-first mentality.
- **Agile Decision-making**
- **Quick Response:** In the face of rapidly changing customer demands, agility in decision-making ensures that the organization can pivot its strategies effectively.
- **Empowering Frontline Employees:** Those who directly interact with customers are often best placed to understand their demands. Leaders empower these frontline employees to make decisions that enhance customer satisfaction.

Integrating Technology

- **Data Analytics:** By harnessing data analytics, leaders can glean insights into customer behavior, preferences, and pain points, enabling them to forecast and meet emerging demands.
- **Digital Solutions:** Leveraging digital platforms and tools can enhance the customer experience, streamline service delivery, and offer personalized solutions.

Building Long-term Relationships

- **Beyond Transactions:** Effective leaders view customers not just in terms of transactions but as long-term partners. This perspective prioritizes building trust and loyalty.
- **Open Communication:** Leaders promote open channels of communication with customers, ensuring they feel heard and valued.

Strategic Planning for Evolving Demands

- **Anticipating Trends:** Instead of merely reacting to current demands, visionary leaders anticipate future trends and preferences, positioning their organizations ahead of the curve.

- **Continuous Innovation:** Encouraging a culture of innovation ensures that products, services, and processes evolve in line with changing customer demands.

Leadership in the modern era requires a deep commitment to serving customers' ever-evolving demands. By fostering a culture of responsiveness, leveraging technology, and prioritizing long-term relationships, leaders can ensure their organizations not only meet but exceed customer expectations, driving business growth and sustainability.

Adapting Leadership Styles based on Team Maturity and Capacity

Effective leadership isn't a one-size-fits-all solution; it requires the capacity to gauge and respond to the developmental level of teams or individuals being led. Drawing from Hersey and Blanchard's Situational Leadership model (1969), we can understand how the maturity and capacity of a team or individual affects the leadership style that would be most effective.

Understanding Team Maturity and Capacity

- Maturity is often equated with competence or skill level and the commitment or confidence to achieve a particular task.

- Capacity refers to the potential a team or individual has to develop the necessary skills and competences over time.

Four Leadership Styles of Situational Leadership:

- **Telling (S1):** High-task focus, low relationship focus.
    - Suitable for teams/individuals at a low maturity level, lacking the skills but potentially willing to take on the task.

- **Selling (S2):** High-task focus, high relationship focus.
    - Ideal for individuals or teams that are trying to develop skills but lack confidence.

- **Participating (S3):** Low-task focus, high relationship focus.
    - Best for teams/individuals with the skills required but may be lacking in confidence or motivation.

- **Delegating (S4):** Low-task focus, low relationship focus.
    - Effective for teams/individuals at high maturity levels who possess both the confidence and competence to complete tasks independently.

Mapping Team Maturity & Capacity to Leadership Styles

- **Low Maturity, High Capacity (S1):** Newly formed teams or fresh hires might have high potential but lack specific skills. Here, a directive style, like 'Telling', would be most effective.

- **Growing Maturity, Growing Capacity (S2):** As the team begins acquiring skills but still needs direction, the 'Selling' style becomes apt, providing direction coupled with encouragement.

- **High Maturity, Varied Capacity (S3):** For teams that are skilled but vary in motivation, the 'Participating' style, which involves shared decision-making, is ideal.

- **High Maturity, High Capacity (S4):** When a team is both competent and committed, leaders can delegate tasks and trust the team to handle them efficiently.

Dynamic Nature of Leadership

Recognizing that an individual or team's maturity and capacity isn't static is crucial. Leaders must adapt their styles as teams evolve, ensuring that leadership remains relevant and effective.

Challenges and Opportunities

The biggest challenge in applying situational leadership lies in accurately diagnosing the development level of teams and individuals. However, when done right, it offers the opportunity to foster growth, enhance team cohesion, and boost productivity by tailoring leadership to the team's specific needs.

The essence of situational leadership is adaptability. Leaders who understand the nuances of their team's maturity and capacity, and adjust their leadership style accordingly, are better positioned to guide their teams towards success.

Understand How to Improve Organizational Performance Through the Application of Relevant Leadership and Management Skills

Skill Sets

One of the critical distinctions in organizational theory is the difference between leadership and management. While these roles often overlap, especially in smaller organizations, understanding the unique skill sets associated with each can help in optimizing organizational performance.

Different Skill Sets for Leaders and Managers

- **Leadership Skills:** Leadership is about setting a direction for the organization, aligning people with that direction through communication, and motivating people to action, amongst other responsibilities.

- **Visionary:** Ability to see the bigger picture and set the direction for the future.

- **Inspiration:** Motivating team members to achieve more than they thought possible.

- **Strategic Thinking:** Considering long-term outcomes and setting goals to achieve them.

- **Change Management:** Leading people through changes and ensuring smooth transitions.

- **Empathy:** Understanding and addressing the needs, concerns, and aspirations of team members.

- **Risk-taking:** Being willing to take calculated risks to achieve visionary goals.

- **Innovation:** Encouraging new ideas and ways of doing things.

Management Skills

Management, on the other hand, is about ensuring the day-to-day operations of the organization run smoothly. It involves planning, organizing, directing, and controlling.

- **Planning:** Setting out the detailed steps needed to achieve specific objectives.

- **Organizing:** Ensuring resources (human, material, financial) are appropriately allocated.

- **Time Management:** Ensuring tasks are completed within set timelines.

- **Problem-solving:** Identifying issues and determining the best solutions.

- **Decision Making:** Making choices based on data and the best interest of the organization.

- **Delegation:** Assigning tasks to team members based on their skills and workload.

- **Monitoring and Evaluation:** Regularly checking progress towards goals and making necessary adjustments.
- **Budgeting and Resource Allocation:** Making sure resources are used effectively and efficiently.

The Overlap

While leaders and managers have distinct skill sets, in practice, there's often a significant overlap. For instance:

- A leader might need management skills like decision-making during strategic planning.
- A manager might need leadership skills like empathy when dealing with team challenges.

Organizational performance is optimized when both leadership and management skills are applied effectively. Recognizing the differences and similarities between these skill sets, and harnessing them in tandem, is crucial for sustained success.

Leadership Skills Explained

Vision Creation

One of the fundamental roles of a leader is to provide a clear vision for the organization. This involves:

- **Future Orientation:** Leaders should be forward-thinking, imagining the potential future states of the organization.
- **Inclusivity:** Engage various stakeholders in crafting this vision, ensuring it's both ambitious and achievable.

Setting Direction

This involves:

- **Strategic Alignment:** Aligning the organization's mission, vision, and values with its strategies and goals.
- **Prioritization:** Deciding on the primary objectives and steering the team toward them.

Communication

Effective leaders must be excellent communicators, and this involves:

- **Clarity:** Articulating thoughts, strategies, and expectations in a way that is easily understood.
- **Open Dialogue:** Encouraging feedback, listening to concerns, and addressing them.
- **Consistency:** Ensuring that messages are consistent across all channels and platforms.

Risk-taking

Being a leader often involves making difficult decisions that come with risks. This skill involves:

- **Calculated Decisions:** Weighing the benefits against the potential pitfalls.
- **Resilience:** Bouncing back from failures or setbacks, and using them as learning experiences.

Planning

While often seen as a managerial skill, planning is crucial for leadership too. It encompasses:

- **Strategic Planning:** Mapping out the long-term strategies and actions to achieve the vision.
- **Contingency Planning:** Having backup plans in case the original ones don't work out.

Listening

A skill sometimes overlooked but vital for leadership is the ability to listen. This means:

- **Active Listening:** Paying full attention, understanding, responding, and remembering what is being said.
- **Empathy:** Understanding and sharing the feelings of another, building trust.

Decision Making

Leaders often have to make challenging decisions that affect the entire organization:

- **Analytical Thinking:** Breaking down complex problems and understanding their components.
- **Stakeholder Consideration:** Taking into account how decisions impact all stakeholders, not just a select few.

A comprehensive leadership role requires a balance of these skills. While some may come naturally to certain individuals, all can be developed and honed over time. Being effective in these areas not only propels the organization forward but also motivates and inspires the team to achieve their best.

Managerial Skills Explained

Team Building

This is the ability to:

- **Recruitment & Selection:** Identify and bring in the right talent that aligns with organizational goals.
- **Motivation:** Foster a positive and encouraging environment, ensuring everyone feels valued.
- **Conflict Resolution:** Address and mediate any team disputes to maintain harmony.

Team Leadership

This includes:

- **Role Modeling:** Demonstrating the behaviors and work ethic expected of the team.
- **Support:** Providing resources and tools that team members need to succeed.
- **Feedback:** Offering regular, constructive feedback to help team members grow and improve.

Communication

Effective managers are adept communicators:

- **Clarity:** Clearly convey tasks, expectations, and feedback.
- **Active Listening:** Ensure they understand team feedback and concerns.
- **Regular Updates:** Keep the team informed about broader organizational goals and changes.

Time Management

Managers must:

- **Prioritize:** Decide what tasks are most important and tackle those first.
- **Schedule:** Use tools and strategies to allocate time effectively.
- **Avoid Procrastination:** Address tasks promptly to avoid last-minute rushes.

Meeting Deadlines

This involves:

- **Planning Ahead:** Breaking projects into tasks and setting interim deadlines.
- **Resource Allocation:** Ensuring the team has the resources they need when they need them.
- **Accountability:** Holding oneself and the team accountable for meeting set timelines.

Performance Management

Key aspects include:

- **Goal Setting:** Establish clear, measurable objectives for each team member.
- **Regular Check-ins:** Review performance regularly and adjust as necessary.
- **Development Plans:** Identify areas of growth and offer opportunities for skill enhancement.

Delegation

Effective managers

- **Trust:** Rely on their team's skills and expertise.
- **Task Assignment:** Assign tasks based on team members' strengths and capabilities.
- **Follow-up:** Check in periodically without micromanaging.

Project Management

This skill set encompasses:

- **Project Planning:** Define the scope, objectives, and deliverables.
- **Risk Management:** Identify potential roadblocks and devise strategies to mitigate them.
- **Monitoring:** Keep track of progress and make adjustments as needed.

Problem Solving

Managers often face challenges that require:

- **Analytical Thinking:** Break problems into parts to understand them better.
- **Creative Solutions:** Think outside the box for innovative solutions.
- **Decision Making:** Choose the best solution based on available data.

While leadership and management often overlap, the roles and skills required can be distinct. Managers are more focused on getting things done effectively and efficiently, ensuring that teams are cohesive, and tasks are completed. Mastery of these managerial skills ensures smoother operations and contributes significantly to organizational success.

Improving Organisational Performance through Leadership and Management Skills: Motivation

- **Content Theories of Motivation:** These theories delve into what people's needs are and how these needs motivate them.

- **Maslow's Hierarchy of Needs:** Maslow proposed that people are motivated by five basic categories of needs: physiological, safety, love/belonging, esteem, and self-actualization. According to him, as each need is met, individuals become motivated by the next need in the hierarchy.

- **Herzberg's Two-Factor Theory:** Herzberg identified two sets of factors that influence motivation in the workplace:

- **Hygiene factors:** These are factors that can demotivate if they are not present but do not necessarily motivate when they are (e.g., salary, working conditions).

- **Motivational factors:** These are factors that truly motivate when present (e.g., achievement, recognition).

- **McClelland's Theory of Needs:** McClelland believed in three major needs:
    - Achievement: A drive to excel.
    - Power: The need to coach and guide others.
    - Affiliation: The need for friendly relationships.

- **Alderfer's ERG Theory:** Alderfer condensed Maslow's five needs into three categories:
    - Existence: Deals with our basic material requirements.
    - Relatedness: Our relationships with others.
    - Growth: Our development as a person.

Process Theories of Motivation
These theories provide an understanding of how various factors affect our motivation and how they interact.

- **Vroom's Expectancy Theory:** According to Vroom, motivation is a product of three variables: expectancy (belief that effort will lead to performance), instrumentality (belief that performance will lead to outcomes), and valence (value or importance one places on the outcome).

- **Locke's Goal Setting Theory:** Locke proposed that setting specific and challenging goals led to higher levels of performance. The key components of this theory are goal specificity, goal difficulty, and feedback.

- **Adam's Equity Theory:** Adams believed that employees are motivated when they perceive that they are treated equitably in comparison to others. This theory stresses the importance of fairness and balance in the workplace.

A deep understanding of motivational theories and their practical application can significantly improve organizational performance. Leaders and managers can leverage these theories to develop strategies that address the specific needs and aspirations of their workforce. By addressing both content and process aspects of motivation, organizations can create an environment where employees are driven to perform at their best.

Influence on Commitment, Energy, Cooperation, and Engagement Through Leadership and Management Skills

Commitment

Commitment in the workplace signifies an employee's passion and loyalty towards their work and the organization.

How motivation influences commitment

When employees see that their needs (as described in Maslow's and Alderfer's theories) are being met, or when they perceive fairness in their roles (as per Adams' Equity Theory), their commitment to the organization increases. Specific and challenging goals, as per Locke's theory, can also bind employees to a commitment to achieving those goals.

Energy

Energy refers to the zeal, enthusiasm, and vigor with which employees approach their tasks.

How motivation influences energy

The intrinsic motivation stemming from Herzberg's motivational factors or McClelland's need for achievement can drive an employee to approach tasks with increased energy. Moreover, when employees believe that their efforts will result in desired outcomes (Vroom's Expectancy Theory), their energy levels to achieve those results rise.

Cooperation

Cooperation in the workplace refers to the collaborative efforts of employees in achieving common goals.

How motivation influences cooperation

The need for affiliation, as described by McClelland, emphasizes the human need for friendly relationships and collaboration. When employees feel that their efforts are equitably rewarded and recognized (Adam's Equity Theory), there's an increased drive to cooperate and collaborate with colleagues.

Engagement

Engagement refers to the emotional connection and involvement an employee has with their job and organization.

How motivation influences engagement

When employees' basic and psychological needs are met (Maslow's Hierarchy), they feel more connected to their job roles. Similarly, goals that are clear and challenging (Locke's Goal Setting Theory) can lead to increased job engagement. The perception that one's efforts are leading to significant outcomes (as per Vroom's Expectancy Theory) also increases engagement.

The application of leadership and management skills rooted in a strong understanding of motivation theories can significantly influence employees' commitment, energy, cooperation, and engagement. By recognizing and addressing the intrinsic and extrinsic motivators that drive individual employees, leaders and managers can foster a more positive, productive, and cohesive work environment.

How Leaders Motivate and Practical Aspects of Motivation

Collaborative Working:

- **Description:** Collaborative working is when individuals, teams, or different departments come together to share knowledge and ideas, working towards a shared goal.
- **How Leaders Motivate Through It:** Leaders who prioritize collaboration often create a sense of unity and shared purpose. They frequently facilitate brainstorming sessions, team meetings, and cross-functional projects that emphasize collective intelligence over individual achievements.

Shared Understanding

- **Description:** This refers to ensuring that everyone in the team understands and is aligned with the organization's goals, values, and mission.
- **How Leaders Motivate Through It:** By creating a shared understanding, leaders ensure that every team member knows their role and the importance of their contributions. Leaders often hold alignment meetings, workshops, or town halls to communicate and reinforce these shared objectives.

Constructive Feedback

- **Description:** Constructive feedback is specific, helpful, and positive criticism that aids in understanding areas of improvement.
- **How Leaders Motivate Through It:** Leaders who provide regular, constructive feedback ensure that employees know their strengths and areas for growth. This not only helps in personal and professional development but also creates a culture where continuous improvement is valued.

Learning and Development

- **Description:** This pertains to providing opportunities for employees to acquire new skills or knowledge, enhancing their professional growth.

- **How Leaders Motivate Through It:** Leaders committed to the continuous learning of their teams often invest in training programs, workshops, or courses. By doing so, they signal that they value and are willing to invest in the growth of their employees, leading to higher morale and motivation.

Inspiring

- **Description:** Leaders inspire by setting a vision that excites and motivates the team towards achieving something bigger than themselves.
- **How Leaders Motivate Through It:** Inspirational leaders lead by example. They are often the embodiment of the values and vision of the organization. Through their passion, commitment, and dedication, they inspire others to push boundaries and achieve greatness.

Creating an Environment

- **Description:** This involves cultivating a workplace culture that supports, encourages, and nurtures its employees.
- **How Leaders Motivate Through It:** A supportive environment is one where employees feel safe to voice their opinions, take risks, and be their authentic selves. Leaders foster such environments by promoting open communication, inclusivity, and ensuring that the well-being of employees is prioritized.

Motivation is not a one-size-fits-all solution. What motivates one individual might not motivate another. Effective leaders understand this diversity of needs and adjust their approach accordingly. By fostering collaboration, ensuring shared understanding, providing feedback, encouraging continuous learning, inspiring the team, and creating a nurturing environment, leaders can substantially elevate the motivation and performance of their teams.

Performance Management

Performance management is a systematic process that involves various activities intended to enhance an organization's efficiency by ensuring that the performance of individuals and teams aligns with the organization's goals and strategies. Central to effective performance management is the clarity of desired end results and proper goal setting.

Importance of Clarity in End Results

- **Alignment with Organizational Objectives:** Clear end results ensure that individual and team efforts are directed towards achieving the broader objectives of the organization.

- **Measurement and Accountability:** Clearly defined results provide a benchmark against which actual performance can be measured, ensuring accountability.

- **Reduced Ambiguity:** When end results are clear, it reduces uncertainties and ambiguities, leading to more focused efforts and minimized wasted resources.

Effective Goal Setting in Performance Management

SMART Criteria:

- **Specific:** Goals should be clear and unambiguous, outlining exactly what is expected.
- **Measurable:** Outcomes should have criteria for measuring progress and achievement.
- **Achievable:** While goals should be challenging, they should also be attainable given the available resources and constraints.
- **Relevant:** The goals set should align with the broader objectives and priorities of the organization.
- **Time-bound:** Each goal should have a clear timeframe for completion.

Regular Monitoring and Feedback

It's essential not just to set goals but to regularly monitor progress towards them. Regular check-ins and feedback sessions help in course correction and ensure that efforts remain aligned.

Inclusion in the Goal-setting Process

Involve employees in the goal-setting process. When individuals participate in setting their own goals, they're more likely to be committed and motivated to achieve them.

Flexibility

While goals provide direction, it's important to maintain some flexibility. Changes in the external environment or within the organization might necessitate adjustments to goals.

Challenges in Clarity of End Results and Goal Setting

- **Changing Organizational Priorities:** Organizations can shift directions based on market conditions, making it challenging to maintain clear and constant end results.

- **Ambiguous Communication:** If organizational goals and strategies are not communicated clearly, it can lead to misalignment in end results.

- **Lack of Resources:** Sometimes, even with clear end results, the necessary resources (like time, funds, or manpower) might not be available to achieve them.

Performance management, anchored on the clarity of end results and robust goal-setting practices, is pivotal for organizational success. It not only ensures alignment of efforts but also provides direction, motivation, and a sense of purpose to the workforce. Properly implemented, it can significantly enhance the effectiveness and productivity of an organization.

Agreement with Staff

Reaching an agreement with staff is a foundational aspect of human resource management and plays a pivotal role in ensuring organizational harmony, clarity of roles, and productivity. These agreements can range from formal contracts to informal understandings, but they all serve as a bridge between management and employees to clarify expectations, responsibilities, and benefits.

Purpose of Agreement with Staff

- **Clear Expectations:** Agreements spell out the responsibilities and expectations for both the employer and the employee. This clarity minimizes confusion and disputes in the future.

- **Legal Protection:** Formal agreements, like employment contracts, offer legal protection to both parties in case of disputes or conflicts.

- **Stability:** Agreements provide a sense of stability and assurance to employees about their roles, remuneration, and job security.

- **Role Definition:** Clearly outlines job descriptions, roles, and responsibilities.

Components of a Staff Agreement

- **Job Description:**
  - A clear outline of the employee's duties, responsibilities, and the expectations associated with their role.

- **Terms of Employment:**
  - Details about employment type (full-time, part-time, temporary), work hours, probation periods, and other specifics.

- **Compensation and Benefits:**
  - Details about salary, bonuses, benefits (healthcare, retirement, etc.), and other compensations.

- **Workplace Policies:**
  - Clauses related to organizational policies like code of conduct, harassment, leave policies, etc.

- **Confidentiality and Non-compete Clauses:**
  - Terms related to the protection of organizational secrets and restrictions on employees joining competitors after leaving the organization.

- **Termination Clauses:**
  - Stipulations about notice periods, reasons for termination, severance pay, etc.

Importance of Regular Reviews and Updates

- **Changing Business Needs:** As the organization evolves, the terms of the staff agreement may need adjustments to suit current business realities.

- **Legal Updates:** Employment laws and regulations change over time. Regularly updating agreements ensures compliance with current laws.

Negotiation and Agreement

Engaging in constructive negotiation is often necessary to reach a mutually beneficial agreement. Open communication, understanding each other's concerns, and working collaboratively are keys to successful negotiation.

Challenges in Reaching Agreement

- **Diverse Expectations:** Sometimes, employers and employees have different expectations, leading to prolonged negotiations.

- **Economic Constraints:** Economic realities, like budgetary constraints, can limit an organization's ability to meet all employee demands.

- **Legal Complexities:** Navigating the intricacies of employment laws can be challenging, especially in multinational contexts.

Reaching an agreement with staff is not just a formality but an essential step to foster mutual respect, clarity, and cooperation. Effective agreements serve as a roadmap, guiding both the organization and its employees towards mutual success. Properly implemented, they play a crucial role in building a motivated, clear-headed, and productive workforce.

Reward

Reward systems are fundamental components of an organization's human resource strategy, designed to recognize and remunerate employees' contributions. Effective reward systems not only motivate and retain employees but also align their efforts with organizational goals.

Purpose of Reward Systems

- **Motivation:** Rewards can serve as a significant motivator, encouraging employees to put in more effort and achieve higher performance.
- **Retention:** Competitive reward systems help organizations retain top talent by ensuring they feel valued for their contributions.
- **Attraction:** An attractive reward package can lure top-tier candidates during recruitment processes.
- **Reinforcement:** Rewarding specific behaviors reinforces those behaviors, directing employees towards desired organizational outcomes.
- **Equity:** Ensures that there's fairness in how employees are compensated, leading to reduced feelings of inequity and dissatisfaction.

Types of Rewards

a. Financial Rewards

- **Salary and Wages:** Regular payment based on employee role and responsibility.
- **Bonuses:** One-off payments based on performance or achievement of specific milestones.
- **Profit Sharing:** A share of the company's profits given to its employees.
- **Stock Options**: Offering employees shares or options at a discounted price.

b. Non-financial Rewards

- **Recognition:** Public or private acknowledgment of an employee's achievements.

- **Promotions:** Moving an employee to a role with more responsibilities, typically accompanied by increased pay and privileges.

- **Additional Leave:** Providing extra paid time off as a reward.

- **Flexible Work Hours:** Allowing employees flexibility in their work schedules.

- **Training and Development:** Offering courses or further education to aid in personal and professional growth.

Key Considerations in Designing Reward Systems

- **Alignment with Organizational Goals:** Rewards should steer employees towards outcomes beneficial to the organization.
- **Fairness:** It's crucial that rewards are perceived as fair to prevent dissatisfaction and potential conflicts.
- **Transparency:** Clear communication regarding how rewards are determined can eliminate misunderstandings.
- **Flexibility:** As organizational needs and market conditions change, reward systems should also adapt.
- **Cost-effectiveness:** Rewards should be sustainable and within the budgetary constraints of the organization.

Challenges in Reward Management

- **Subjectivity:** Rewards based on subjective evaluations can lead to perceptions of bias.
- **Inflation:** Regular adjustments to financial rewards are necessary to account for inflation.
- **Cultural Differences:** Multinational organizations need to consider cultural differences in perceptions of rewards.
- **Balancing Short-term vs. Long-term Goals:** Rewards should not just focus on immediate achievements but also long-term growth and sustainability.

Rewards play a pivotal role in shaping employee behavior, motivation, and overall organizational culture. By recognizing and valuing contributions, organizations can create a positive, high-performance environment that not only achieves business objectives but also nurtures and grows its most valuable asset – its people.

Performance Monitoring and Measurement

Performance monitoring and measurement are critical components of effective management. They help organizations ensure that they're moving towards their goals efficiently and allow for adjustments when they're not. Properly implemented, they can drive both individual and organizational success.

The Importance of Performance Monitoring and Measurement:

- **Accountability:** Ensures that all members of the organization are held responsible for their actions and contributions.
- **Feedback:** Provides a mechanism for regular feedback, helping employees understand where they stand and what's expected.
- **Decision-making:** Offers data-driven insights to inform decisions at all levels of the organization.
- **Alignment with Objectives:** Helps ensure that efforts are aligned with the organization's strategic objectives.
- **Identification of Strengths and Weaknesses:** Helps to identify areas of strength and where improvement is needed.

Components of Performance Monitoring and Measurement

a. **Key Performance Indicators (KPIs):** These are specific and measurable metrics that reflect an organization's goals. They might include sales figures, customer satisfaction scores, or any other pertinent metric.
b. **Performance Reviews:** Regular evaluations, often annually, where employees' performances are discussed and feedback is given.
c. **Benchmarking:** Comparing an organization's performance against industry peers or best practices to determine its standing.
d. **Real-time Monitoring:** Using software tools or other systems to monitor performance in real-time, often used in sectors like IT or production.

Best Practices

- **Set Clear and Measurable Objectives:** Performance metrics should be directly tied to clear organizational goals.
- **Ensure Transparency:** All stakeholders should understand how performance is measured and what the expectations are.
- **Regularly Review and Adjust:** Performance metrics should be reviewed regularly to ensure they remain relevant.
- **Use a Mix of Quantitative and Qualitative Measures:** Numbers tell one story, but qualitative insights can provide a fuller picture.
- **Ensure Feedback is Constructive:** The aim is to improve, not to chastise.

Challenges in Performance Monitoring and Measurement

- **Subjectivity:** Even with clear metrics, there can be subjective elements in performance evaluations.
- **Data Overload:** With numerous metrics and vast amounts of data, pinpointing what's important can be challenging.
- **Resistance to Being Measured:** Some employees might resist being constantly monitored or evaluated.
- **Short-term Focus:** Overemphasis on immediate results can sometimes sideline long-term objectives.

Performance monitoring and measurement are not just about oversight but about guiding an organization towards its goals. When done right, they empower organizations to stay on course, make necessary adjustments, and ultimately succeed in their objectives. Effective performance management combines data-driven insights with a human touch, recognizing that numbers only tell part of the story.

Gathering Feedback

Feedback is a crucial aspect of continuous improvement in any organization, helping to shape strategies, refine processes, and enhance relationships with stakeholders. The process of gathering feedback, when done methodically and constructively, can lead to transformative change.

The Importance of Gathering Feedback

- **Continuous Improvement:** Feedback provides insights into areas of improvement and highlights strengths.
- **Stakeholder Engagement:** It engages employees, customers, and other stakeholders, making them feel valued and heard.
- **Decision Making:** Informed decisions can be made based on direct feedback from those affected.
- **Risk Mitigation:** Early feedback can identify potential issues before they escalate.

Methods of Gathering Feedback

a. **Surveys and Questionnaires:** These are structured tools that can gather feedback on specific topics. They can be administered online, on paper, or even verbally.
b. **Focus Groups:** Small, diverse groups discuss specific topics in-depth, providing qualitative insights.
c. **One-on-One Interviews:** Personal interviews allow for deep dives into individual perspectives.

d. **Suggestion Boxes:** Anonymously allows stakeholders to provide insights or raise concerns.
e. **Digital Platforms:** Tools like feedback widgets on websites, or apps designed for feedback collection.
f. **Observational Methods:** Monitoring how stakeholders interact with a product, service, or environment.

Best Practices in Gathering Feedback

- **Clarity:** Ensure questions are clear and unbiased.
- **Anonymity:** Protecting the identity of respondents can lead to more honest feedback.
- **Act on Feedback:** Demonstrating that feedback leads to action encourages future participation.
- **Diverse Methods:** Use various methods to gather comprehensive feedback.
- **Regularly Scheduled Feedback:** Annual reviews, quarterly surveys, etc., ensure consistent feedback.
- **Open-ended Questions:** Allow respondents to share in-depth thoughts and suggestions.

Challenges in Gathering Feedback

- **Response Bias:** Some might only respond when they have extreme opinions, potentially skewing results.
- **Overwhelming Amounts of Feedback:** Large amounts of feedback can be challenging to process and act upon.
- **Ambiguity:** Vague feedback can be hard to interpret and act on.
- **Fear of Repercussions:** Some might be hesitant to give negative feedback if they fear backlash.

Analyzing and Using Feedback

Once feedback is collected, it's essential to analyze it methodically. This can involve quantitative analysis, such as calculating averages or finding trends in survey results, or qualitative analysis, such as thematic coding of open-ended responses. The results should be shared with relevant stakeholders and be used as a foundation for decision-making.

Feedback is a mirror that reflects the realities of an organization. It provides insights that can be the catalyst for growth, change, and innovation. Gathering feedback is not just about collecting data; it's about building stronger relationships with stakeholders and continually striving for excellence.

Use of Data and Outputs

The increasing ubiquity of data in today's organizations highlights the importance of its strategic utilization. Properly gathered and analyzed data can provide insights, drive decisions, and enhance performance. The outputs, or the tangible results from the data analysis, can guide managerial and operational actions.

Purpose of Data and Outputs in Organizations

- **Informed Decision-Making:** Data provides evidence that can make decision-making more objective and outcome-oriented.

- **Performance Monitoring:** Through data, organizations can monitor and measure their performance against set benchmarks or KPIs (Key Performance Indicators).

- **Predictive Analysis:** Data can be used to predict future trends, allowing organizations to be proactive.

- **Customer Insights:** Data can offer insights into customer behaviors, preferences, and pain points.

Effective Use of Data

- **Data Collection:** The first step involves gathering relevant data. This can come from internal sources (like sales figures) or external sources (like market research).

- **Data Cleaning:** Ensuring data is accurate and free from errors is crucial. Any anomalies or mistakes can skew results.

- **Data Analysis:** Using statistical tools or software to glean insights from the data.

- **Data Visualization:** Presenting data in graphs, charts, or dashboards to make it easily understandable.

- **Data Storage:** Storing data securely, ensuring it's accessible for future use and complies with data protection regulations.

Making Sense of Outputs

Outputs refer to the results or findings derived from data analysis. These can include:

- **Reports:** Detailed documents outlining findings.
- **Dashboards:** Visual tools that display data metrics in real-time.
- **Presentations:** Summaries of data findings for stakeholders.
- **Action Plans:** Strategies or steps derived from data insights.

Applying Outputs in Decision-Making

- **Strategic Planning:** Data outputs can guide the direction an organization chooses to take.
- **Operational Improvements:** Insights from data can highlight operational inefficiencies.
- **Risk Management:** Data can identify potential risks, allowing for proactive management.
- **Resource Allocation:** Data can indicate where resources (like time or money) should be spent for maximum impact.

Challenges in Using Data and Outputs

- **Data Overwhelm:** The sheer volume of data can be daunting.
- **Data Security Concerns:** Ensuring data is stored securely and isn't vulnerable to breaches.
- **Interpretation Errors:** Misinterpreting data can lead to incorrect conclusions.
- **Resistance to Data-Driven Decision Making:** Some may prefer traditional methods over data-backed approaches.

In the modern business landscape, data isn't just a by-product of operations; it's a valuable asset that, when used effectively, can drive growth, innovation, and competitive advantage. Properly analyzed and applied outputs enable organizations to navigate complexities with increased clarity and confidence.

Job Design and Characteristics in Relation to Employee Needs

Job design is the structuring of a job role to align with both organizational objectives and the needs and abilities of the individual. It encompasses the specific tasks an employee is responsible for, the methods used in completing these tasks, and the ways in which jobs relate to other roles in the organization. A well-designed job can boost employee motivation, performance, and satisfaction, while addressing their intrinsic and extrinsic needs.

Key Concepts in Job Design

- **Task Variety:** Incorporating a range of tasks to maintain interest and challenge.
- **Task Identity:** Giving employees a whole and identifiable piece of work, enabling them to see the tangible outcomes of their efforts.
- **Task Significance:** Ensuring the task has a substantial impact on others or the organization.
- **Autonomy:** Granting employees freedom, independence, and discretion in scheduling their work and determining procedures.

- **Feedback:** Providing clear, actionable feedback about performance directly from the job.

Employee Needs Addressed through Job Design

- **Intrinsic Needs:**
    - **Competence:** Employees want to feel competent in their roles. Designing jobs that match their skill sets and provide opportunities for growth can meet this need.
    - **Self-determination:** Autonomy in job roles fosters a sense of ownership and control, fulfilling the need for self-determination.
    - **Meaningfulness:** Jobs that have significance and align with personal values can cater to the need for meaningful work.

- **Extrinsic Needs:**
    - **Security:** Clear job roles, responsibilities, and stable employment can address the need for job security.
    - **Recognition:** Jobs that have built-in feedback mechanisms or opportunities for acknowledgment can cater to the need for recognition.
    - **Work-life balance:** Flexible job designs can help employees balance their professional and personal lives.

Job Characteristics Model (Hackman & Oldham)

This model suggests that five core job dimensions lead to three critical psychological states, resulting in beneficial personal and work outcomes:

- **Core Job Dimensions:** Task variety, task identity, task significance, autonomy, and feedback.

- **Psychological States:** Experienced meaningfulness, experienced responsibility for outcomes, and knowledge of the actual results.

- **Outcomes:** High intrinsic motivation, job satisfaction, quality work performance, and low absenteeism and turnover.

Considerations in Job Design:

- **Technological advancements:** The role of automation and AI in shaping job tasks.

- **Diversity and inclusion:** Designing roles that are inclusive and do not marginalize any group.

- **Ergonomics:** Considering the physical design of jobs, such as workstation design or tool placement.

- **Flexibility:** Offering options like remote work, flexible hours, or job sharing.

Job design is crucial in creating roles that not only fulfill organizational goals but also cater to the diverse needs of employees. An effective job design ensures higher motivation, better performance, reduced turnover, and overall better workplace well-being.

Understand How Leaders and Managers Utilize Teams in Improving Organisational Performance

Characteristics of High-Performing Teams

Shared Purpose and Established Goals

A hallmark of high-performing teams is a united vision or purpose. This means every member of the team understands and is committed to the team's mission, purpose, or objective. The team's goals are clearly defined, agreed upon, and are aligned with the organization's broader objectives. The sense of purpose serves as the guiding light for the team, ensuring that everyone is moving in the same direction.

Effective Communication

Open, transparent, and frequent communication is crucial in high-performing teams. Team members feel free to express their ideas, concerns, and feedback without fear of reprisal. Clear communication reduces misunderstandings, fosters collaboration, and ensures that everyone remains informed.

Mutual Trust and Respect

Trust is the foundation of any successful team. Team members trust each other's competence and count on each other to deliver. They respect individual strengths, value diversity, and understand that every member plays a pivotal role in the team's success.

Complementary Skills

In high-performing teams, members have a diverse set of skills that complement one another. This ensures that the team has the necessary expertise and capabilities to handle a wide range of challenges and tasks. It fosters a sense of interdependence, where members rely on each other's unique skills and expertise.

Accountability and Responsibility

Each member of a high-performing team is accountable for their tasks and responsibilities. They take ownership of their roles, ensuring that they meet their commitments and deliver results. Team members hold each other accountable, which further ensures that everyone stays on track.

Positive Team Dynamics

Team members collaborate effectively, handle conflicts constructively, and support one another. There's a balance between professional focus and interpersonal rapport, creating a conducive atmosphere for both work and camaraderie.

Adaptive and Flexible

High-performing teams can quickly adapt to changes and are resilient in the face of challenges. They are flexible in their approach, willing to pivot when needed, and can navigate through uncertainties efficiently.

Regular Feedback and Continuous Improvement

Such teams have mechanisms for regular feedback. They review their performance, learn from mistakes, and continuously strive to improve. They are committed to personal and collective growth.

Strong Leadership

Effective teams often have a leader who provides direction, inspires, and supports the team. The leader also ensures that the team has the necessary resources and removes any obstacles hindering the team's performance.

Aligned with Organizational Culture

The team's values, norms, and behaviors align with the broader organizational culture. This alignment ensures that the team's efforts are in sync with the company's mission and values.

High-performing teams are not just about bringing together skilled individuals. It's about fostering a collaborative environment where members trust each other, communicate effectively, and are committed to a shared purpose. Leaders and managers can harness the potential of such teams to drive significant improvements in organizational performance.

Clear Roles in High-Performing Teams

In the context of high-performing teams, the importance of well-defined roles cannot be overstated. The delineation of clear roles and responsibilities is instrumental in achieving team cohesion, ensuring efficient task execution, and mitigating potential conflicts. Let's delve deeper into the significance of clear roles in teams:

Elimination of Ambiguity

When team members have clear roles, there is no ambiguity about who is responsible for what. This clarity reduces the potential for tasks to be overlooked or duplicated.

Streamlined Workflow

Clearly defined roles ensure that there's a systematic approach to task execution. Workflows are more streamlined as every team member knows what they're supposed to do and when they're supposed to do it.

Enhanced Accountability

When roles are clearly delineated, there's a heightened sense of responsibility and ownership. Team members are more likely to take initiative and be accountable for their tasks, leading to a higher quality of work.

Efficient Use of Skills and Expertise

With specific roles, team members can leverage their strengths and expertise to the fullest. This specialization leads to quicker task completion and higher quality outputs.

Reduced Conflicts

Role clarity mitigates the chances of team members stepping on each other's toes. When everyone knows their boundaries, potential conflicts due to overlapping responsibilities are reduced.

Enhanced Communication

When roles are clear, communication becomes more targeted. Team members know whom to approach for specific queries or concerns, leading to quicker problem resolution.

Clear Decision-making Path

In situations that require quick decisions, having well-defined roles means everyone knows who holds the authority to make specific decisions, leading to swift action.

Support and Collaboration

With clear roles, team members can easily identify whom to turn to for support or collaboration on specific tasks. This fosters a collaborative environment where team members assist and complement each other's efforts.

Goal Alignment

Clear roles ensure that everyone's individual efforts are aligned towards the team's collective goals. Each member knows their part in the bigger picture, reinforcing the importance of their contribution.

Continuous Growth and Development

When roles are set, individuals can focus on honing their specific skills and expertise, leading to personal and professional development.

Clear roles form the backbone of a high-performing team. They provide structure, enhance efficiency, and foster a culture of accountability and collaboration. Leaders and managers must invest time and resources in establishing and communicating these roles to maximize team performance.

Strong Interdependencies in High-Performing Teams

Interdependency in a team context refers to the reliance team members have on one another to achieve common goals. In high-performing teams, strong interdependencies are vital for driving collaboration, promoting synergy, and ensuring successful task completion. Let's explore the significance and features of strong interdependencies in teams:

Mutual Reliance for Success

Strong interdependencies mean that each team member's success is contingent upon the contributions of others. This mutual reliance fosters a sense of shared responsibility and commitment to the team's objectives.

Enhanced Collaboration

When team members recognize that their outputs are reliant on inputs from others, they are more inclined to collaborate. They actively seek feedback, share information, and work collectively to solve problems.

Increased Accountability

Understanding the dependence on one's role can increase personal accountability. Team members know that if they don't deliver, it could impede the performance of others and, by extension, the entire team.

Shared Resources and Skills

Interdependent teams often share resources, knowledge, and skills. This pooling of capabilities leads to diverse solutions and innovative approaches to challenges.

Synergy Creation

The idea that the collective output of a team can exceed the sum of individual contributions is rooted in interdependency. This synergy allows high-performing teams to achieve more than individuals working in isolation.

Efficient Workflow Management

In interdependent teams, tasks are often sequenced in a manner where one member's output serves as another's input. This sequencing can streamline workflows and minimize bottlenecks.

Strengthened Communication

Due to the interconnected nature of their tasks, interdependent teams typically develop strong communication structures. They prioritize open dialogue to ensure everyone remains aligned and informed.

Conflict Resolution

Interdependencies can sometimes lead to disagreements. However, high-performing teams use these as opportunities for growth. Their mutual reliance drives them to proactively address and resolve conflicts.

Flexible Role Adaptation

While roles might be defined, strong interdependencies often require team members to adapt and support each other during peak workloads or unforeseen challenges.

Builds Trust

Working closely and depending on one another fosters trust. Team members learn to believe in the reliability and integrity of their colleagues, leading to stronger team cohesion.

Strong interdependencies are a hallmark of high-performing teams. They transform individual contributors into a cohesive unit, driven by mutual goals and shared responsibilities. For leaders and managers, fostering interdependencies can be a strategic tool to elevate team performance and collaboration.

Agreed Decision Making Process in High-Performing Teams

Every team, irrespective of its size or purpose, makes decisions. Whether it's about project direction, resource allocation, or conflict resolution, the decision-making process is critical. High-performing teams differentiate themselves by having a clear, agreed-upon decision-making process. This shared process fosters unity, clarity, and efficiency. Below is an exploration of the importance and features of an agreed decision-making process in teams:

Consistency and Predictability

When teams have a standardized decision-making process, members know what to expect. This consistency can expedite decisions and reduce the anxiety or uncertainty that can sometimes accompany them.

Transparency and Trust

A clear process illuminates how and why decisions are made. This transparency can build trust among team members, as they understand that decisions aren't arbitrary but are based on a consistent method.

Reduced Conflicts

Conflicts often arise due to perceived inequities or misunderstandings. A well-defined decision-making process minimizes these by providing a structured, fair mechanism for making choices.

Engaging All Voices

High-performing teams often prioritize inclusivity. An agreed decision-making process ensures that all members have an opportunity to voice their opinions and concerns, leading to more comprehensive and well-considered decisions.

Efficient Use of Time

Instead of debating how to make a decision, teams can focus on the decision itself, which is a more productive use of their time.

Clear Roles and Responsibilities

A structured decision-making process often designates roles (e.g., facilitator, note-taker, final decision-maker). This clarity can streamline the process and ensure all aspects are addressed.

Flexibility in Approach

While the process is standardized, it's not rigid. High-performing teams understand that different situations might require tweaks or adjustments. The key is that any deviations are agreed upon and understood by all.

Learning and Iteration

After decisions are made, the team reflects on the process's effectiveness. Was every voice heard? Was the decision effective? This reflective practice allows teams to continually refine their approach.

Accountability and Ownership

Decisions made through a shared process are more likely to be supported by the entire team. This collective buy-in ensures that members feel accountable for the decision's outcomes, leading to greater ownership and commitment.

Facilitation of Complex Decisions

Complex decisions that involve multiple stakeholders, abundant data, and high stakes can be daunting. An agreed-upon process provides a roadmap, guiding the team step-by-step.

An agreed decision-making process is not about bureaucracy or red tape; it's about facilitating smooth, effective, and inclusive decisions. For high-performing teams, this process is less about the mechanics and more about the shared values of clarity, inclusivity, and collective ownership. It's an essential tool for leaders and teams aiming for excellence in collaboration and outcomes.

Use of Review and Feedback in High-Performing Teams

Feedback and regular reviews are vital components that contribute to the success of high-performing teams. They act as guiding tools, helping teams understand their strengths, identify areas of improvement, and fostering a culture of continuous growth and development. Here's a comprehensive look at the significance of review and feedback for these teams:

Foster Continuous Improvement

Regular feedback ensures that teams are always aware of their performance standards and areas needing enhancement.

Enhance Performance and Productivity

Constructive feedback aids team members in understanding their roles better and identifying the specific areas where they excel or require further development.

Strengthen Team Relationships

Honest and open feedback fosters trust among team members. When teams are accustomed to giving and receiving feedback, they cultivate a culture of transparency and mutual respect.

Reinforce Positive Behaviors

Recognizing and appreciating positive behaviors encourages team members to continue performing well. It acts as positive reinforcement.

Address and Correct Negative Behaviors

Constructive feedback provides an opportunity to address undesirable behaviors or actions in a non-confrontational manner.

Clarify Roles and Responsibilities

Regular reviews can help clarify any misunderstandings regarding roles and responsibilities, ensuring that all members are aligned with the team's objectives.

Encourage Personal and Professional Growth

Feedback often includes insights into training needs or areas for professional development. This not only benefits the individual but also enhances the overall skill set of the team.

Facilitate Decision Making

Reviews provide a platform for team members to discuss challenges and opportunities. Collective feedback can guide the decision-making process, ensuring that it's holistic and well-informed.

Create a Learning Environment

When teams embrace feedback, they create a learning culture. Mistakes are seen as opportunities for growth, and successes become benchmarks for excellence.

Boost Team Morale and Engagement

Recognizing the hard work and achievements of team members through feedback can significantly boost morale. Engaged teams are more motivated, committed, and likely to go the extra mile.

Enhance Goal Alignment

Reviews often involve revisiting team and organizational goals. Feedback ensures that all team members are aligned with these objectives and working cohesively towards them.

Identify Opportunities and Threats

Regular feedback loops can highlight potential opportunities for innovation or areas where the team might face threats or challenges.

The use of review and feedback is not merely a formality but a strategic tool for high-performing teams. It helps maintain a pulse on team dynamics, ensures alignment with organizational goals, and promotes a culture of excellence and continuous improvement. Effective leaders understand the power of feedback and make it an integral part of their team's operations.

Stable Team Membership in High-Performing Teams

Stable team membership is a pivotal aspect of high-performing teams, providing consistency and cohesion to a group's dynamic. A stable team membership means that team members have been together for a considerable period, allowing them to develop deeper working relationships and better understand each other's strengths, weaknesses, and working styles. Below, we delve into the significance and benefits of stable team membership for high-performing teams:

Fosters Trust and Cohesion

With time, team members learn to trust one another, making them more willing to share ideas, take risks, and be open about their concerns.

Efficient Communication

Long-standing team members develop a shorthand for communication, understanding nuances, and contexts which might be missed by newer members. This streamlines discussions and decision-making.

Builds Collective Memory

Teams with stable membership have a shared history, which means they can draw from past experiences, successes, and mistakes. This collective memory aids in faster decision-making and problem-solving.

Reduces Onboarding Time

Frequent changes in team composition necessitate continual onboarding and orientation, consuming time and resources. Stable teams can dive straight into tasks without the need for regular inductions.

Enhances Role Clarity

Over time, team members settle into their roles and responsibilities, ensuring that everyone knows what is expected of them, leading to better task distribution and minimal overlaps.

Predictability and Reliability

With stable membership, team members can predict and rely on each other's reactions and behaviors, which aids in planning and executing tasks more efficiently.

Encourages Skill Specialization

As team members stay together longer, they can specialize in their roles, leading to deepened expertise and higher quality of work.

Boosts Team Morale

Knowing that they are part of a stable team where members have their back can boost individual morale, leading to a more positive team atmosphere.

Reduces Conflicts

Familiarity among stable team members can reduce misunderstandings and conflicts. Even when disagreements arise, long-standing members have a better understanding of resolving them constructively.

Enhances Collective Accountability

Stable teams have a greater sense of collective ownership and accountability for their projects, leading to better outcomes.

Facilitates Long-term Planning

Leaders can plan long-term strategies and projects more effectively when they are assured of a stable team membership.

Strengthens Organizational Culture

When team membership remains consistent, it becomes easier to instill and maintain a strong team and organizational culture.

Stable team membership isn't just about retaining employees; it's about building a foundation for team success. It provides a platform for individuals to grow together, understand each other deeply, and work in a harmonious rhythm that can significantly enhance team performance. Effective leaders recognize the value of team stability and strive to create environments where teams can remain consistent and thrive.

Strong Learning Environment in High-Performing Teams

A strong learning environment is characterized by a culture that prioritizes, encourages, and supports continuous learning and growth for all team members. It's an environment where mistakes are viewed as learning opportunities, feedback is frequent and constructive, and everyone is motivated to enhance their skills and knowledge. The presence of such an environment can substantially bolster a team's performance, adaptability, and innovation. Here's why a strong learning environment is crucial for high-performing teams:

Fosters Adaptability

In today's rapidly changing world, the ability to adapt to new technologies, markets, or methods is crucial. Teams that are always learning are better prepared to pivot when necessary.

Promotes Continuous Improvement

In a strong learning environment, there's a perpetual emphasis on improving processes, products, or services. This consistent focus on enhancement translates to better outcomes and performance.

Nurtures Innovation

Teams that are encouraged to learn tend to be more curious and experimental. They'll often bring new ideas to the table, fostering an innovative spirit within the organization.

Enhances Problem-Solving Skills

Exposure to varied learning resources and methodologies equips team members with a diverse set of tools and perspectives to approach challenges, making them adept problem solvers.

Builds Confidence and Competence

Continuous learning enhances the competence of team members. As they grow more skilled, their confidence in handling complex tasks or projects also rises.

Facilitates Skill Diversification

A team where each member is encouraged to learn can boast of a diverse skill set, making it multifaceted and versatile.

Reduces Skill Gaps

Regular training and upskilling ensure that no member lags in the required skills, ensuring uniformity in the team's competence level.

Encourages Open Communication

A learning environment usually promotes open dialogue. Teams are more inclined to discuss, debate, and share, leading to better collaboration.

Supports Career Growth

Personal development is a critical motivator for many professionals. By fostering a learning environment, organizations show that they care about their employees' career trajectories, leading to higher retention rates.

Bolsters Resilience

Teams accustomed to a learning mindset are more resilient. They view setbacks as learning opportunities rather than failures, making them more persistent and less likely to get demotivated.

Promotes a Growth Mindset

Cultivating a learning environment encourages a growth mindset, where challenges are embraced, and the potential for development is acknowledged.

Enhances Competitive Advantage

Teams that are consistently up-to-date with the latest industry trends, technologies, and methodologies are better positioned to outperform competitors.

Incorporating a strong learning environment within teams is more than just offering training programs. It's about creating a culture where curiosity is celebrated, growth is prioritized, and every experience—good or bad—is valued as a learning opportunity. High-performing teams thrive in such environments because they're consistently evolving, adapting, and pushing the boundaries of what they can achieve. Leaders play a pivotal role in fostering this environment by setting the right tone, providing necessary resources, and championing the cause of continuous learning.

Team-Based Rewards System

A team-based rewards system recognizes and incentivizes the collective efforts of a team rather than solely focusing on individual contributions. Such a system emphasizes collaboration, mutual accountability, and the shared successes of a team. When effectively implemented, team-based rewards can foster a more cohesive, motivated, and high-performing team environment.

Key Features of a Team-Based Rewards System

- **Collective Metrics:** The primary basis for rewards is the collective performance of the team, measured through metrics like team targets, project completion rates, or customer satisfaction scores.
- **Equitable Distribution:** Rewards, whether monetary or non-monetary, are distributed equally among team members to emphasize collective success.
- **Balanced with Individual Rewards:** While the focus is on the team, it's essential to strike a balance to ensure individual efforts and expertise are also acknowledged.

Advantages of Team-Based Rewards

- Fosters Collaboration: Such a system emphasizes the importance of working together and pooling resources and talents for a common goal.
- Promotes Collective Accountability: Team members feel a shared responsibility for the team's successes and failures, leading to a sense of mutual accountability.
- Reduces Unhealthy Competition: By rewarding collective outcomes, the system can minimize internal competition and potential conflicts among team members.
- Encourages Knowledge Sharing: Since the success of one is tied to the success of all, team members are more likely to share knowledge, resources, and expertise.
- Supports Organizational Objectives: By aligning team goals with broader organizational objectives, the entire team works in harmony with the organization's direction.

Challenges and Considerations

- **Free-Riders:** There's a risk that some team members might coast on the efforts of others, benefiting from the team's success without contributing equally.
- **Complexity in Measurement:** Determining collective metrics that fairly represent a team's effort can be challenging.
- **Potential for Conflict:** Differences in opinions on effort and contribution can lead to internal conflicts if not managed well.

- **Balancing Act:** It's crucial to ensure that team-based rewards don't overshadow individual achievements, which could demotivate high-performing individuals.

Best Practices for Implementation

- **Clear Communication:** Ensure that the team understands the criteria for rewards, how they're measured, and how they align with broader organizational goals.
- **Combine with Individual Rewards:** Maintain a balance between team-based and individual rewards to recognize all forms of contributions.
- **Regular Feedback:** Provide teams with regular feedback on their performance, ensuring they're aligned with the set objectives.
- **Periodic Review:** Periodically review and adjust the rewards system to keep it relevant and effective.
- **Encourage Peer Recognition:** Allow team members to recognize and celebrate the contributions of their peers.

A team-based rewards system can be an excellent tool for fostering collaboration and promoting a unified approach to achieving objectives. However, it's essential to implement it thoughtfully, considering the unique dynamics and needs of the organization and its teams.

Team Leadership

Team leadership goes beyond simply managing people. It's about creating a cohesive unit that can function independently and cohesively, driving results that align with organizational objectives. Effective team leadership is a dynamic combination of various roles, strategies, and processes.

Roles and Models of Team Leadership

- **The Visionary:** Sets the long-term vision for the team, providing a clear sense of direction and purpose.
- **The Coach:** Focuses on individual and collective development, ensuring that team members grow in their roles.
- **The Mediator:** Handles conflicts and ensures a harmonious team environment.
- **The Decision Maker:** Makes key choices, especially when the team is unsure of the next steps.
- **The Communicator:** Ensures that all team members are informed, valued, and heard.

Establishing the Culture of Team Performance

- Shared Values and Beliefs: Cultivating a common set of values and beliefs that guide team behaviors and decisions.

- Celebrating Diversity: Recognizing and valuing the unique contributions of each team member.

- Open Communication: Encouraging honest, transparent, and consistent communication among team members.

Setting Clear Aims and Objectives

Clearly defining what the team is working towards ensures alignment with the organizational goals. This involves setting SMART (Specific, Measurable, Achievable, Relevant, Time-bound) goals that provide clarity and focus.

Establishing Reporting Lines

Clearly delineated reporting structures ensure accountability, smooth workflow, and efficient communication.

Celebrating Success

Regularly acknowledging and rewarding team achievements boosts morale, motivation, and commitment.

Managing Conflict

- **Open Dialogue:** Addressing issues head-on through open discussions.
- **Neutral Mediation**: Introducing a third-party mediator when conflicts escalate.
- **Conflict Resolution Training:** Equipping team members with skills to manage and resolve conflicts independently.

Communication, Collaboration, and Team Decision Making

- **Regular Team Meetings:** Scheduled touchpoints to discuss progress, address issues, and make collective decisions.
- **Collaborative Tools:** Utilizing tools and platforms that foster collaboration, such as shared document platforms or project management software.
- **Democratic Decision Making:** Ensuring that all voices are heard and considered in decision-making processes.

Creativity of Teams

Promoting brainstorming sessions, encouraging diverse thinking, and providing a safe environment where innovative ideas are valued and explored.

Monitoring Performance and Measuring Team Success

- **Performance Metrics:** Establishing clear KPIs (Key Performance Indicators) to gauge team performance.
- **Regular Reviews:** Holding periodic reviews to assess performance against set objectives.

- **Feedback Mechanisms:** Implementing channels for feedback, both from team members and external stakeholders.

Empowerment

Delegating authority, equipping team members with the necessary resources, and trusting them to make decisions can lead to increased ownership, accountability, and productivity.

Team leadership is multifaceted and dynamic. It requires leaders to wear multiple hats, from visionary to mediator, to ensure the team's success. By focusing on clear communication, goal setting, and empowerment, team leaders can guide their teams towards achieving remarkable results.

Development of Teams: Stages of Team Development

The concept of team development has been widely studied, and among the models proposed, Tuckman's stages of group development remains one of the most referenced. Other scholars like Honey, Leigh, and Maynard have also contributed to the understanding of this field. Here's an overview:

Tuckman's Stages of Group Development

Dr. Bruce Tuckman introduced this model in 1965, which he refined over the years. It outlines the path that most teams follow on their way to high performance. The stages are:

Forming:

- Team members get to know each other.
- Uncertainty about roles and the team's objectives.
- Dependency on the leader for guidance and direction.

Storming:

- Conflicts arise as team members start to voice out opinions.
- There's competition for status and acceptance of individual differences.
- The leader might be challenged.

Norming:

- Team members start to work more cohesively.
- Development of mutual respect.
- More cooperative, developing their own standards and rules.

Performing:

- Team members are now competent, autonomous, and able to handle the decision-making process without supervision.
- The team is more strategically aware and knows clearly why it's doing what it's doing.

Adjourning (added later):

- The team completes its mission or project.
- Members move on to other activities.
- Recognition for a job well done.

Honey and Mumford's Learning Styles

While Peter Honey and Alan Mumford are more recognized for their work on individual learning styles, their research provides insights that can be applied to team development. By understanding the different learning preferences within a team (Activist, Reflector, Theorist, and Pragmatist), leaders can ensure a well-rounded approach to tasks and problem-solving, ultimately enhancing team performance.

Leigh and Maynard's Teamwork Cycle

Leigh and Maynard identified five stages in their Teamwork Cycle, emphasizing the importance of review and feedback at every stage:

- **Identify the need for teamwork:** Recognize the situation that requires a collective approach.

- **Select appropriate members:** Based on skills, experience, and fit with the team's culture.

- **Plan and prepare:** Establish clear goals, roles, and processes.

- **Act:** Implement the plan, with members fulfilling their respective roles.

- **Review and feedback:** Continuously evaluate the team's progress and adjust as necessary.

Understanding the various stages of team development and the dynamics at play can help leaders guide their teams more effectively, ensuring they progress from formation to high performance. Each model provides unique insights, but when combined, they offer a holistic perspective on team development and performance.

Team Performance

Team performance isn't just about the collective output of the group; it's also a reflection of how individual members come together, leveraging their unique skills and backgrounds, towards a common objective. Here's a deeper dive into the intricacies of team performance:

Utilizing Skills of Individual Members

- Strength in Diversity: Every member brings a unique set of skills, knowledge, and experience. Harnessing these differences enriches the team's problem-solving ability and fosters innovative solutions.

- Role Allocation: Assign tasks based on individual strengths. This ensures that each task is handled by someone competent, increasing the efficiency and quality of output.

Shared Goals and Ambitions

- **Unified Vision:** A clear and shared goal ensures that everyone is moving in the same direction. It provides purpose and meaning to the team's efforts.
- **Alignment with Organizational Goals**: When team objectives align with the broader organizational aims, it creates a synergy where the success of the team amplifies the success of the entire organization.

Working With and Supporting Colleagues

- **Collaborative Environment:** Foster an environment where members feel free to share ideas, voice concerns, and seek help.
- **Emotional Intelligence:** Understand and respect the emotions of team members. This builds trust and enhances collaboration.

Wanting Success for the Team

- **Collective Mindset:** Instill a sense of collective ownership where successes (and failures) are shared by the entire team.
- **Celebrating Achievements:** Regularly recognize and celebrate the team's accomplishments to boost morale and motivation.

Common Understanding of the Plan

- **Transparent Communication:** Ensure everyone understands the project's objectives, the strategy to achieve them, and their individual roles within that framework.
- **Feedback Loops:** Regularly update the team on progress and changes, and encourage feedback to continuously refine the plan.

Individual Performance and Its Impact

- **Accountability:** Every team member's performance can significantly impact the entire team. Hence, fostering a sense of responsibility is crucial.
- **Peer Reviews:** Peer assessments can offer insights into individual contributions and how they affect the group. This can help in identifying areas of improvement and leveraging strengths.

High-performing teams are not just about achieving objectives but about the journey of getting there. It's about how members collaborate, support each other, and leverage individual strengths for collective success. Building such a team requires understanding, patience, and consistent effort from both leaders and members.

Team Performance: The Consequences of Underperformance

Team performance directly correlates with an organization's success. When teams underperform, it can have a cascading negative impact on the overall health and objectives of the organization. Below, we delve into the repercussions and manifestations of underperforming teams:

Negative Impact on Organizational Performance

- **Reduced Productivity:** Inefficient teams often struggle to complete tasks on time, leading to delayed projects and missed deadlines.
- **Financial Implications:** Delays, reworks, and inefficiencies can increase costs and diminish the return on investment.

Goals Not Achieved

- **Missed Objectives:** An underperforming team often falls short of meeting its targets, which can have a domino effect on dependent departments or projects.
- **Reputation Damage:** Consistent failure to meet goals can tarnish the organization's reputation in the eyes of stakeholders, clients, and even potential hires.

Blame Culture

- **Deflection Over Reflection:** Instead of identifying root causes and addressing them, members might resort to blaming peers for failures.
- **Eroded Trust:** A culture of blame can lead to reduced trust among team members, further weakening team cohesion.

Conflict

- **Interpersonal Disputes:** Underperforming teams often have unresolved tensions that can escalate into larger conflicts.
- **Decreased Morale:** Persistent conflicts can lead to a toxic work environment, decreasing overall team morale.

Staff Absence

- **Increased Sick Days:** A stressful, conflict-ridden environment can contribute to increased absenteeism due to health reasons or to avoid the workplace.
- **Mental Health Concerns:** Prolonged exposure to such environments can also lead to anxiety, depression, and other mental health issues among team members.

Retention Issues

- **High Turnover:** Discontented team members may seek opportunities elsewhere, leading to a high attrition rate.
- **Recruitment Challenges:** A known culture of underperformance and conflict can deter potential high-quality recruits.

The ramifications of team underperformance extend beyond missed objectives. It can erode the very fabric of an organization's culture, leading to a vicious cycle of conflict, absenteeism, and high turnover. Addressing these issues requires proactive leadership, timely interventions, and a commitment to fostering a positive, collaborative team environment.

Team Performance: Navigating the Landscape of Remote and Virtual Teams

Remote and virtual teams have become increasingly prevalent, especially in the wake of the global shift towards digital transformation and the necessity of remote work during the COVID-19 pandemic. However, these teams come with their unique set of challenges and advantages. Here's an in-depth look:

Working in Real-Time

- **Time Zone Differences:** With members potentially spread across the globe, coordinating synchronous activities can be challenging.

- **Immediate Feedback:** Real-time collaboration tools like video conferencing and instant messaging can facilitate quicker decision-making.

Communication

- **Common Message:** Ensuring all team members understand and align with the project's goals and updates is crucial.
- **Over-communication:** In a virtual setting, it's often better to over-communicate than to risk misunderstandings or assumptions.

Clarity and Direction

- **Lack of Clarity:** Without face-to-face interactions, instructions can sometimes be misinterpreted, leading to confusion.
- **Second Guessing:** Team members might question their understanding or the intent behind messages, causing hesitation in decision-making.

Empathy and Personal Connection

- **Lack of Personal Interaction:** Virtual teams often miss the informal chats and bonding that occur naturally in physical offices.
- **Building Relationships:** Virtual team-building activities and regular check-ins can help bridge this gap and foster connections.

Work Ethic and Cultural Differences

- **Varied Work Patterns:** Different time zones mean members work at different times, possibly leading to overlaps or gaps.
- **Cultural Nuances:** With members from diverse backgrounds, understanding and respecting cultural norms is vital for harmony.

Hidden Incompetence

- **Less Visibility:** It can be harder to spot underperformance or areas of improvement in a virtual environment.
- **Regular Check-ins:** Managers should hold consistent one-on-ones to gauge performance and provide feedback.

Productivity Concerns

- **Potential Diminished Productivity:** Distractions at home or lack of a structured work environment can hinder efficiency.
- **Flexible Schedules:** Allowing flexible work hours can help team members choose their most productive times.

Availability

- **24/7 Accessibility:** With digital tools, there might be an unintended expectation of constant availability.
- **Boundaries:** It's essential to set clear work hours and respect off-time to prevent burnout.

While remote and virtual teams offer flexibility and access to a global talent pool, they also come with their set of challenges. Effective leadership, clear communication, and a deep understanding of the nuances of remote work are vital to harnessing the potential of these teams and ensuring optimal performance.

Frameworks in Team Performance: A Deep Dive into Organizational Policy, Managerial Support, and Culture

Organisational Policy and Procedures

Organisational policies and procedures serve as the backbone for any company. They provide guidelines that ensure consistency, clarity, and fairness throughout the organization. For teams, especially remote and virtual ones, these can play a pivotal role:

- **Clear Expectations:** Clearly defined policies mean that every team member knows what's expected, minimizing misunderstandings.
- **Procedure Consistency:** With a set way of doing things, there's less room for error and miscommunication, particularly crucial for virtual teams that might not have real-time opportunities to clarify doubts.
- **Conflict Resolution:** Having established procedures in place ensures that when conflicts arise, there's a predefined path to resolution.

Managerial Support

A supportive management can be the difference between a flourishing team and one that struggles:

- **Open Communication:** Managers who are approachable and foster open channels of communication make it easier for team members to share concerns and suggestions.

- **Empowerment:** A supportive manager empowers their team, giving them the tools, resources, and autonomy they need to succeed.

- **Growth and Development:** Managerial support often translates to opportunities for professional growth, training, and development for team members.

- **Feedback Mechanism:** Supportive managers not only provide constructive feedback but are also open to receiving feedback, ensuring a two-way street of communication.

Organizational Culture

Culture, often described as the "way things are done around here," is intangible but has a palpable impact on teams:

- **Collaborative Spirit:** A culture that values collaboration will naturally have teams that work well together, sharing ideas and resources freely.

- **Recognition and Rewards:** In cultures where achievement is recognized and celebrated, team morale is typically higher.

- **Flexibility and Adaptability:** Cultures that are open to change and encourage adaptability often find it easier to navigate challenges, especially in the dynamic world of remote work.

- **Trust and Integrity:** A culture built on trust means fewer oversight and micromanagement, crucial for remote teams where constant monitoring isn't feasible.

Conclusion

Recap of Key Themes and Insights

Throughout this book, we have embarked on a comprehensive exploration of the multifaceted nature of strategic leadership and management within organizations. Our journey has taken us through the foundational concepts, theories, and practical applications that are essential for anyone looking to excel in leadership roles. Here, we revisit the critical themes and insights that have been covered, reinforcing the core principles that underpin effective leadership and management.

The Essence of Strategic Leadership and Management

We began by delving into the essence of strategic leadership and management, emphasizing their pivotal role in guiding organizations towards achieving their long-term objectives. Strategic leadership was discussed not merely as a position of authority but as a dynamic process that involves vision, influence, and the strategic alignment of organizational goals. We explored how effective management complements leadership by focusing on the operational aspects of achieving these goals, highlighting the symbiotic relationship between the two.

Dynamics of Relationships within Organizations

Understanding the dynamics of relationships within organizations emerged as a crucial theme. We examined how the interplay between leaders, followers, and the organizational context shapes the culture and performance of an organization. The importance of communication, trust, and mutual respect was underscored, along with the need for leaders to recognize and address the diverse needs and motivations of their team members.

Leadership and Management Theories and Styles

A significant portion of the book was dedicated to dissecting various leadership and management theories and styles. From transactional to transformational leadership, situational leadership to contingency theory, and beyond, we evaluated how these frameworks offer different lenses through which to view the challenges and opportunities inherent in leading and managing. The exploration of these theories provided insights into how leaders can adapt their approach to suit the unique demands of their organizational environment and the individuals they lead.

Adapting Styles to Different Situations

The necessity for leaders to adapt their styles to different situations was a recurring theme. We discussed how organizational life cycles, from start-ups to mature enterprises, and specific challenges, such as crisis management or navigating rapid market changes, require leaders to be flexible and responsive. The ability to adjust one's leadership style based on the context and needs of the team is essential for fostering resilience and ensuring sustained organizational success.

Improving Organizational Performance

Finally, we highlighted the critical importance of improving organizational performance through the strategic application of leadership and management skills. Practical strategies for creating a compelling vision, building cohesive teams, managing performance effectively, and fostering an environment of motivation and engagement were discussed. These strategies are designed to equip leaders with the tools they need to not only inspire their teams but also to drive tangible improvements in organizational performance.

As we reflect on these themes, it becomes clear that effective strategic leadership and management are not static disciplines but rather evolving practices that require continuous learning, adaptation, and application. The insights provided in this book aim to serve as a foundation upon which leaders and managers can build their capabilities, enhance their understanding, and ultimately lead their organizations to greater heights of achievement and success.

The Importance of Continuous Learning and Adaptation

In the rapidly evolving landscape of modern business, the ability to continuously learn and adapt is not just an advantage—it is a necessity for leaders and managers aiming for success. This section underscores the critical importance of embracing continuous learning and demonstrating adaptability and flexibility in leadership roles.

Commitment to Continuous Learning and Personal Development

The pace of change in technology, market dynamics, and global economic factors demands that leaders not only keep up but stay ahead. Continuous learning and personal development are the bedrock upon which leaders can build their ability to lead effectively in such an environment. This commitment involves actively seeking out new knowledge, skills, and experiences that can enhance one's leadership capabilities. It includes everything from formal education and training to informal learning opportunities such as mentorship, coaching, and experiential learning through new projects and challenges.

Leaders and managers who dedicate themselves to continuous learning are better equipped to foresee trends, innovate, and apply new strategies to drive their organizations forward. Moreover, by embodying the value of learning, they set a powerful example for their teams, fostering a culture of curiosity, innovation, and resilience.

Adaptability and Flexibility in Leadership

Adaptability and flexibility are the hallmarks of effective leadership in today's business world. These qualities are crucial for navigating the complexities and uncertainties that characterize modern organizational environments. Adaptability refers to the ability of leaders to adjust their strategies, approaches, and behaviors in response to changing circumstances. Flexibility involves the willingness to consider alternative perspectives and solutions, even when they diverge from traditional or previously successful methods.

Leaders who demonstrate adaptability and flexibility are capable of leading their organizations through change with agility and confidence. They are skilled at managing transitions, whether it involves shifting market conditions, organizational restructuring, or adopting new technologies. By remaining open to change and prepared to pivot when necessary, adaptable leaders can seize opportunities, mitigate risks, and guide their organizations to success in an unpredictable world.

The importance of these qualities cannot be overstated. They enable leaders to respond effectively to challenges, lead their teams through periods of uncertainty, and capitalize on new opportunities that arise. Adaptability and flexibility also foster a more innovative and inclusive organizational culture, where diverse ideas and approaches are valued, and where experimentation and learning from failure are seen as essential to growth.

The commitment to continuous learning and the cultivation of adaptability and flexibility are indispensable for leaders and managers in the 21st century. These qualities not only enhance individual leadership effectiveness but also contribute to the overall resilience, agility, and success of organizations.

Practical Application of Concepts

The exploration of strategic leadership and management theories, along with the rich insights into adaptability, team dynamics, and performance improvement, forms a robust foundation for enhancing leadership effectiveness and organizational performance. This section aims to bridge the gap between theory and practice, providing guidance on how these concepts can be applied in real-world settings.

Bringing Theories to Life

Understanding leadership and management theories is one thing; applying them effectively in the day-to-day management of organizations is another. Leaders and managers can enhance their effectiveness by:

Adapting Leadership Styles: Recognizing the specific needs of your team and organizational context to adapt your leadership style accordingly. For instance, employing a more directive style in crisis situations while adopting a transformational approach when fostering innovation and change.

Leveraging Motivational Theories: Applying insights from motivational theories to develop strategies that enhance employee engagement and productivity. This might involve tailoring incentive programs to match the intrinsic and extrinsic motivators of your team members.

Implementing Performance Management Techniques: Utilizing performance management strategies discussed to set clear expectations, provide meaningful feedback, and drive continuous improvement within your teams.

Reflection and Integration

For theories and strategies to be truly effective, they must be reflected upon and integrated into one's leadership approach. Leaders are encouraged to:

Reflect on Current Practices: Take time to assess your current leadership and management practices. Identify areas where the application of new strategies could lead to improved outcomes.

Seek Feedback: Engage with peers, mentors, and team members to gain feedback on your leadership style and its impact. Use this feedback as a basis for continuous improvement.

Experiment and Learn: Be open to experimenting with different leadership styles and strategies. The application of theory to practice is often a trial-and-error process, where learning from failures and successes is paramount.

Case Studies and Real-World Examples

One effective way to understand the practical application of leadership and management concepts is through case studies and real-world examples. These narratives can provide valuable insights into how other leaders have navigated challenges, applied theories, and adapted their strategies to achieve success. Reflecting on these examples can inspire new approaches and ideas for your own leadership practice.

Developing a Personal Action Plan

To facilitate the integration of insights gained from this book into your leadership approach, consider developing a personal action plan. This plan could outline specific goals, strategies, and actions you intend to take to enhance your leadership effectiveness and organizational performance. Regularly review and adjust this plan as you gain new insights and experiences.

The practical application of the concepts discussed in this book is crucial for transforming theory into effective leadership and management practices. By encouraging reflection, adaptation, and the continuous integration of new insights, leaders can enhance their effectiveness and drive organizational success. As you move forward, let the principles and strategies explored serve as a guide, inspiring you to lead with confidence, creativity, and a deep commitment to continuous improvement.

The Role of Teams in Achieving Organizational Success

The success of an organization is increasingly dependent on its ability to foster high-performing teams. In today's complex and interconnected business environment, the collective effort, creativity, and innovation of a team often outweigh the capabilities of any single individual. This section emphasizes the critical role teams play in organizational success and outlines strategies for building, leading, and maximizing the potential of these teams.

Building High-Performing Teams

High-performing teams are characterized by a shared vision, strong collaboration, and a commitment to achieving common goals. Building such teams requires a deliberate effort to:

Select Diverse Team Members: Diversity in skills, perspectives, and backgrounds enhances creativity and problem-solving capabilities. Leaders should strive to assemble teams that bring a broad range of experiences and viewpoints to the table.

Establish Clear Objectives and Roles: Every team member should understand the team's overall objectives and how their individual roles contribute to achieving these goals. Clarity in expectations and responsibilities is crucial for team cohesion and effectiveness.

Cultivate a Trusting Environment: Trust is the foundation of any high-performing team. Leaders can foster trust by encouraging open communication, demonstrating reliability and competence, and showing respect for team members' contributions and perspectives.

Understanding Team Dynamics

The dynamics within a team—how team members interact, communicate, and work together—significantly influence its performance. Leaders need to be adept at:

Navigating Conflicts: Conflict is inevitable in teams but, when managed constructively, can lead to better decisions and stronger relationships. Leaders should encourage healthy debate and provide mechanisms for resolving conflicts in a way that strengthens the team.

Promoting Collaboration: Collaboration is enhanced when team members feel valued and know that their contributions are essential to the team's success. Leaders should facilitate collaborative processes and create opportunities for team members to work together effectively.

Supporting Team Development: Teams go through various stages of development, from forming to performing. Leaders must recognize these stages and provide the appropriate support and leadership style at each phase to guide the team towards high performance.

Leveraging the Strengths of Diverse Teams

Diverse teams bring a range of experiences, skills, and perspectives that can significantly enhance problem-solving and innovation. To leverage these strengths effectively, leaders should:

Encourage Inclusivity: Ensure that all team members have the opportunity to contribute and that their ideas are heard and valued. An inclusive environment encourages participation and harnesses the full potential of the team's diversity.

Utilize Strengths-Based Leadership: Identify and capitalize on the unique strengths of each team member. By aligning tasks and roles with individual strengths, leaders can enhance engagement and productivity.

Foster a Culture of Continuous Learning: Encourage team members to learn from each other and from their collective experiences. A culture that values learning and growth can adapt more quickly to challenges and opportunities.

The role of teams in achieving organizational success cannot be overstated. By understanding team dynamics, fostering collaboration, and leveraging the strengths of diverse teams, leaders can build high-performing teams that are capable of extraordinary achievements. As organizations continue to navigate the complexities of the modern business landscape, the ability to cultivate effective teams will remain a crucial determinant of success. Leaders who master the art of team building and management will not only drive their organizations forward but will also contribute to a more dynamic, innovative, and inclusive workplace.

Looking Ahead: The Future of Leadership and Management

As we stand on the threshold of a new era in leadership and management, it's imperative to look ahead and contemplate the future trends that will shape our approach to leading and managing in the decades to come. Technological advancements, globalization, and evolving workforce expectations are set to redefine the landscape of leadership and management. This section explores these trends and offers guidance on how leaders can prepare for the changes ahead.

Technological Advancements

The rapid pace of technological innovation is transforming the way organizations operate, communicate, and compete. From artificial intelligence and machine learning to blockchain and the Internet of Things (IoT), technology is reshaping the business landscape in profound ways. Future leaders must be tech-savvy, not only to leverage these technologies effectively but also to anticipate their impacts on business models, operations, and workforce dynamics. Embracing a culture of innovation and continuous learning will be crucial for staying ahead in this technology-driven world.

Globalization

Globalization continues to connect the world's economies, cultures, and populations more closely than ever before. Leaders must navigate the complexities of operating in a global marketplace, including cultural differences, regulatory challenges, and geopolitical risks. The future of leadership and management will increasingly require a global mindset, with a focus on cross-cultural communication, international collaboration, and strategic thinking that transcends borders.

Evolving Workforce Expectations

The expectations of the workforce are changing, driven by demographic shifts, changing attitudes towards work-life balance, and a growing emphasis on corporate social responsibility. Employees are seeking more than just a paycheck; they are looking for purpose, flexibility, and a commitment to social and environmental sustainability. Future leaders must understand these evolving expectations and adapt their organizational cultures accordingly. This includes fostering a purpose-driven environment, promoting diversity and inclusion, and integrating sustainable practices into the core of the business.

Preparing for the Future

To navigate these changes successfully, leaders must adopt a proactive and visionary approach. This involves:

Staying Informed: Keeping abreast of technological trends, global developments, and shifts in workforce dynamics to anticipate how they might affect your organization.

Fostering Agility: Building flexible and resilient organizations that can quickly adapt to change. This means embracing change as an opportunity for growth and innovation.

Developing Future Leaders: Investing in leadership development programs that cultivate the skills and mindsets needed for the future, including technological proficiency, cultural intelligence, and strategic thinking.

The future of leadership and management promises to be both challenging and exciting. As we look ahead, it's clear that the leaders who will thrive are those who are not only responsive to the current landscape but also actively prepare for future challenges and opportunities. By embracing technological advancements, fostering a global mindset, and adapting to evolving workforce expectations, you can lead your organization towards a successful, sustainable future. Let this be a call to action for all aspiring and established leaders: the future is ours to shape, and by being proactive, visionary, and adaptable, we can navigate the uncertainties of tomorrow with confidence and purpose.

Call to Action for Readers

As we draw this book to a close, it's not just an end but a beginning—the start of your journey towards applying the rich insights and strategies you've encountered. This journey into strategic leadership and management is one of continuous growth and learning. Here, we extend a call to action for you, the reader, to not only ponder the concepts discussed but to actively integrate them into your professional life.

Apply Your Knowledge

The theories, models, and practical strategies detailed in this book are tools at your disposal. We urge you to take these tools and apply them within your organizations and teams. Identify opportunities where strategic leadership can make a difference and implement management practices that drive performance and foster a positive organizational culture. Whether it's adapting your leadership style to meet the needs of your team, leveraging motivational theories to enhance engagement, or employing performance management techniques to achieve goals, each step you take is a move towards becoming a more effective leader.

Engage in Continuous Reflection

Leadership and management are dynamic fields, and what works in one context may not in another. Continuous reflection on your practices, decisions, and their outcomes is vital. Reflect on the successes and challenges you encounter, considering what lessons can be learned and how these insights can inform your future actions. Reflection is a powerful tool for personal and professional growth, enabling you to adapt and thrive in an ever-changing environment.

Experiment and Seek Feedback

Innovation in leadership and management often comes from experimentation. Don't be afraid to try new approaches or strategies that you believe could benefit your team or organization. Some experiments will succeed, and others may not yield the expected results, but each offers valuable learning opportunities. Alongside experimentation, actively seek feedback from peers, mentors, and your team. Feedback is a gift that provides new perspectives and insights, helping you refine your approach and enhance your effectiveness as a leader.

Foster a Culture of Learning and Growth

As you apply the concepts from this book and embark on new leadership and management initiatives, strive to foster a culture of learning and growth within your organization. Encourage your team to engage in continuous learning, share knowledge, and support one another's development. By creating an environment where growth is valued and supported, you not only enhance your team's capabilities but also contribute to a more resilient and adaptive organization.

The journey of strategic leadership and management is ongoing, filled with opportunities for growth, learning, and impact. By taking proactive steps to apply the knowledge and skills acquired from this book, engaging in continuous reflection, experimenting with new ideas, and fostering a culture of learning, you position yourself and your organization for success in the complex landscape of modern business. Let this book be a catalyst for your development as a strategic leader and manager, inspiring you to lead with vision, navigate challenges with resilience, and achieve excellence in all your endeavors.

Final Words of Inspiration

As we conclude this journey together, it's important to pause and reflect on the path that lies ahead. The exploration of strategic leadership and management you've embarked upon is more than an academic exercise—it's a call to action, a challenge to elevate yourself and those around you to new heights. The insights and strategies shared in these pages are not just theories; they are beacons guiding you towards becoming a leader who not only envisions a better future but actively shapes it.

The Power of Impactful Leadership

Remember, the potential to make a meaningful impact in your organization and community lies within you. Leadership is not confined to titles or positions; it's an expression of your ability to inspire, influence, and innovate. Whether you're leading a small team or an entire organization, your actions, decisions, and the example you set can ripple through your workplace, industry, and beyond. Embrace the responsibility that comes with this potential; it's a privilege to lead, to guide others towards achieving shared goals, and to contribute to something larger than oneself.

The Journey of Growth

The path of leadership and management is one of perpetual growth and discovery. With every challenge you face and every success you celebrate, there lies an opportunity to learn, adapt, and evolve. This book has equipped you with tools and frameworks, but the real learning begins with application—when you step into the arena, test your ideas, and refine your approach based on real-world experiences. The journey ahead is unique for each reader, filled with its own set of trials and triumphs. Embrace it with an open heart and a curious mind.

The Transformative Power of Strategic Leadership

Strategic leadership and management have the transformative power to change organizations, shape cultures, and impact lives. As you move forward, carry with you the understanding that your leadership can drive innovation, foster inclusivity, and build resilience. The challenges of today and tomorrow require leaders who are not only strategic in their thinking but also compassionate in their approach—leaders who see beyond the bottom line to the people and communities they serve.

Closing Reflection

As we part ways, take a moment to reflect on the leader you are today and the leader you aspire to become. The journey of leadership is as much about personal transformation as it is about professional achievement. It's a journey that demands courage, commitment, and compassion. But the rewards—a sense of purpose, the growth of those you lead, the success of your organization—are immeasurable.

Let this book be a stepping stone on your path, but remember, the map to your destination is not fixed. It's drawn by your actions, your choices, and your vision. Lead with intention, with empathy, and with the unwavering belief that through effective leadership and management, you have the power to make a significant, lasting impact.

Go forth with confidence, for the future is yours to shape.

www.ingramcontent.com/pod-product-compliance
Lightning Source LLC
Chambersburg PA
CBHW080950290526
45795CB00009B/2951